# A Heart to Hear

*Presented to:*

_____


*From:*

_____

# *Endorsements*

*What a privilege it has been to see Jennifer grow in Christ and to see how she beautifully expresses her thoughts in writing "A Heart to Hear."*

*I am excited and inspired every time I read one of these clear and thought-provoking devotionals. Jennifer speaks openly and honestly about things she and those close to her have dealt with. She encourages me to do better in my walk with Christ.*

— **Sondra Saunders, Senior Preschool and Children's Minister Prestonwood Baptist Church, Plano, TX**

♡ ♡ ♡

*I have had the great blessing of watching Jennifer as she develops into the woman that God has purposed her to be. God's wisdom, love, and grace flow through Jennifer's relevant writing, which empowers each reader to approach life's everyday issues with confidence. Jennifer's heart is to hear her Heavenly Father speak.*

— **Cindy Langley, Women's Ministry Leader Restoration Church, Euless, TX**

♡ ♡ ♡

*"A Heart to Hear" was birthed as a weekly social networking media to ladies and quickly extended beyond her local congregation. Jennifer's ministry of encouragement that is captured in "A Heart to Hear" is positive, inspiring, refreshing, and challenging.*

*Having walked with our Lord since the young age of seven, Jennifer's field lab of six children, a professional consultant husband, a dog, and numerous pets along the way provides ample opportunities to cry out to her Beloved Lord.*

*Regardless of the current season of your life, "A Heart to Hear" invites you to walk a week or two, a year, or more with Jennifer. After all, there were three on the Emmaus Road! You can also visit Jennifer's blog at heart-to-hear.blogspot.com.*

— **Peggy Davis, Former CBA bookseller, Asheville, NC**

# A Heart to Hear

## MEDITATIONS FOR A WOMAN'S HEART

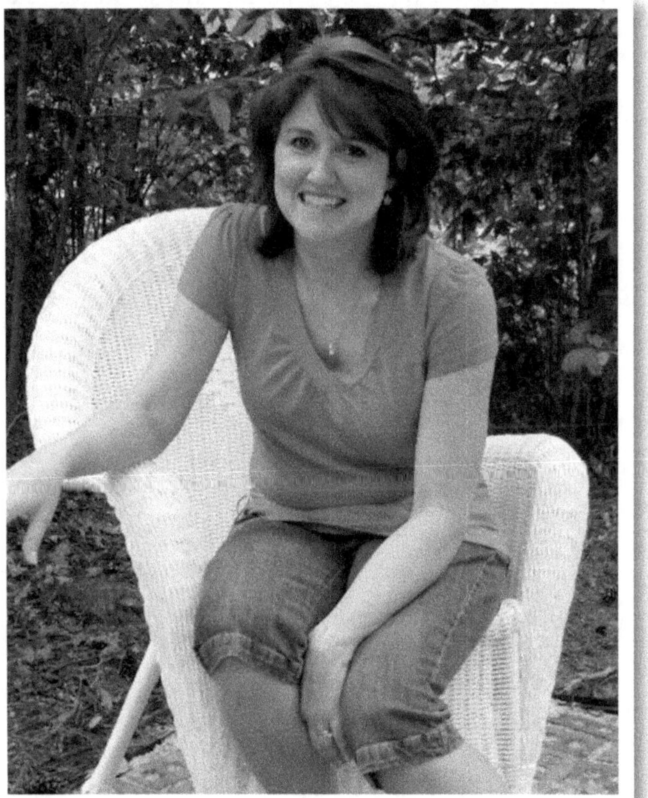

with
Jennifer Churchwell Davis

Unless otherwise notated, all Scriptures in this book are taken from the HOLY BIBLE, NEW INTERNATIONAL VERSION®. Copyright © 1973, 1978, 1984 Biblica. Used by permission of Zondervan. All rights reserved.

Scripture quotations marked (NLT) are taken from the Holy Bible, New Living Translation, copyright © 1996, 2004, 2007 by Tyndale House Foundation. Used by permission of Tyndale House Publishers, Inc., Carol Stream, Illinois 60188. All rights reserved.

"Scripture quotations taken from the Amplified® Bible, Copyright © 1954, 1958, 1962, 1964, 1965, 1987 by The Lockman Foundation. Used by permission." (www.Lockman.org)

# A Heart to Hear
## MEDITATIONS FOR A WOMAN'S HEART
with
Jennifer Churchwell Davis

Copyright © 2011 by Jennifer Churchwell Davis

All rights reserved. This book is protected under the copyright laws of the United States of America. This book may not be copied or reprinted for commercial gain or profit. The use of short quotations or occasional page copying for personal or group study is permitted and encouraged. Permission will be granted on request.

Paperback Book: ISBN-13: 978-0-9826957-5-3

E-Book: ISBN-13: 978-0-9826957-6-0

Edited and designed by Nancy E. Williams with Peggy Davis

Published by LAURUS BOOKS
Printed in the United States of America

**LAURUS BOOKS**
P. O. Box 2464
McDonough, GA 30253
www.LaurusBooks.com

This book is dedicated to my parents,

**Jim and Ethel Churchwell**

From an early age, they taught me to love the Lord and His Word. Dad taught me to make time to read the Word daily, and Mom showed me the joy of sharing the treasures found there with others.

## *Acknowledgements*

I want to thank my husband, Rick, for all he has done to help me learn to walk in freedom in the Lord. Without him, I would not be the person I have become.

In addition, I would like to thank my husband's mom, Peggy Davis. This book would not be in your hands if not for her heart to hear the Lord and to follow His instructions.

Finally and forever, I am completely indebted to my Abba Father and His redeeming love. Apart from Him, I am completely useless.

# Table of Contents

| | | |
|---|---|---|
| Dedication | | ................................. 7 |
| Acknowledgements | | .............................. 9 |
| JAN 1 - 7 | Lay Down Your Heavy Load | ........... 13 |
| JAN 8 - 14 | Relationship, Not Religion | ............ 15 |
| JAN 15 - 21 | The Burden-Bearer. | .................. 17 |
| JAN 22 - 28 | Call To Be Single-minded | ............. 19 |
| JAN 29 - FEB 4 | Find Your Place and Fill It | ............. 21 |
| FEB 5 - 11 | Focus! | ............................ 23 |
| FEB 12 - 18 | Blindsided!. | ....................... 25 |
| FEB 19 - 25 | Draw Near! | ........................ 27 |
| FEB 26 - MAR 4 | Hold On To Your Hope. | ............... 29 |
| MAR 5 - 11 | Who Are You Wearing. | ................ 31 |
| MAR 12 - 18 | Blank Check | ....................... 33 |
| MAR 19 - 25 | Believing Is The Key | ................. 35 |
| MAR 26 - APR 1 | Go with What You Know! | ............. 37 |
| APR 2 - 8 | Pouring Water on Dry Ground | ......... 39 |
| APR 9 - 15 | Don't Let Your Mind Wander | .......... 41 |
| APR 16 - 22 | Change Is Inescapable | ................ 43 |
| APR 23 - 29 | False Perception. | .................... 45 |
| APR 30 - MAY 6 | Fight for Your Freedom | ............... 47 |
| MAY 7 - 13 | Relax and Enjoy the Ride. | ............. 49 |
| MAY 14 - 20 | Stand Still!. | ........................ 51 |
| MAY 21 - 27 | Keep Pressing In | .................... 53 |
| MAY 28 - JUN 3 | I Don't Need Your Help! | ............... 55 |
| JUN 4 - 10 | He's Got Your Back | .................. 57 |
| JUN 11 - 17 | Going On Vacation | .................. 59 |
| JUN 18 - 24 | Heart on Overload. | .................. 61 |

## *Table of Contents*

| | | |
|---|---|---|
| JUN 25 - JUL 1 | Favorite Fluffy Towel | 63 |
| JUL 2 - 8 | You Never Stand Alone | 65 |
| JUL 9 - 15 | Be Faithful | 67 |
| JUL 16 - 22 | Stop Striving | 69 |
| JUL 23 - 29 | Strength Big Enough for Every Challenge | 71 |
| JUL 30 - AUG 5 | Deny Yourself | 73 |
| AUG 6 - 12 | Flourish and Bear Fruit | 75 |
| AUG 13 - 19 | Kudzu | 77 |
| AUG 20 - 26 | Fresh Start | 79 |
| AUG 27 - SEP 2 | Let It Go! | 81 |
| SEP 3 - 9 | Crock Pot or Microwave? | 83 |
| SEP 10 - 16 | Get A Grip! | 85 |
| SEP 17 - 23 | Walking the Tightrope | 87 |
| SEP 24 - 30 | Poison Darts | 89 |
| OCT 1 - 7 | Feeling Weary? | 93 |
| OCT 8 - 14 | Laser-Guided Missile | 95 |
| OCT 15 - 21 | Overcomers in Training | 97 |
| OCT 22 - 28 | Wormy Apples | 99 |
| OCT 29 - NOV 4 | Don't Throw Away Your Confidence | 101 |
| NOV 5 - 11 | Ouch! | 103 |
| NOV 12 - 18 | Whisper or Megaphone? | 105 |
| NOV.19 - 25 | Give Thanks in All Circumstances | 107 |
| NOV 26 - DEC 2 | What I Can Give | 109 |
| DEC 3 - 9 | Roll With It | 111 |
| DEC 10 - 16 | Reconciling the Vision | 113 |
| DEC 17 - 23 | Prepare Him Room! | 115 |
| DEC 24 - 31 | Saying "Goodbye" Is a Gift | 117 |

## *A Heart to Hear*

### JANUARY 1 - 7
# Lay Down Your Heavy Load

One of my primary roles in life is that of Chief Tidy Upper. I walk through the house picking up things that aren't where they should be and taking them to their proper location. It doesn't take long before I'm juggling multiple items and my fingers are getting cramps as I bend over to pick up yet another misplaced something. When my hands are totally full, I sometimes use my feet, perhaps to retrieve that sock peeping out from under the sofa. It's ridiculous, but I hate the idea of making more than one trip, so I'm always convinced I can carry one more thing.

The Lord showed me recently that I have been applying this approach not only to my home, but to my family and, sometimes, even to my friends. I have cast myself in the role of Chief Tidy Upper of their lives. I have taken personal responsibility for all of their stuff and tried to make everything as neat and tidy as I can, smoothing out relational wrinkles and stashing baggage out of sight.

Last week, the Lord spoke to me very clearly and directly in a dream early one morning. He said, "Your hands are full of many things, but what I desire for you is peace." As I thought about those words, I saw myself staggering around under a load that was never mine to bear. Making things right

## A Heart to Hear

in the lives of my family members or friends is not my job. It is His. My role is simply to lay every burden at the feet of my Abba Father and wait on Him. He will perfect that which concerns me. He delights to redeem and transform. As I wait on Him in trust and peace, I will be transformed, too!

*Abba Father, give us grace to come to You today, in full confidence of Your love and acceptance. Help us commit to You all the ones we love and their needs. Help us walk through this day with hearts full of Your peace.* ♡

# *A Heart to Hear*

### JANUARY 8 - 14
# Relationship, Not Religion

God is calling us to a relationship, not a religion! There is comfort for the flesh in a ritual. You know what is expected, and it is simply a matter of going through the motions. The thought that an unknown God can be pleased by this lets you off the hook for dealing with who you really are. You do your part and hope He does His, which is to bless you as you go your own way.

But the True and Living God has never been content with being unknown. He loves us, and He wants us to know Him. In Philippians 1:9 Paul says, "And this is my prayer: that your love may abound more and more in knowledge and depth of insight …" Paul is talking about a love that knows, sees, and has deep insight. That is the nature of His love for us, and that is the kind of love He longs for us to have for Him.

How precious it is to have friends who truly know us and love us deeply. Our Abba Father wants that depth of relationship with us. Look at how He originally designed life in the Garden of Eden. God came daily to spend time with Adam and Eve. He wanted to be with them. Over and over throughout the Bible, you see God reaching out to individuals. Look at Abraham. God came to Him and said, "I want to make a covenant with you." The Most High God wants relationship

## A Heart to Hear

on a one-on-one basis. He says, "Come, be real with Me. I already know the truth about you. I can heal you. I can restore you. I can make your life worth living." Jesus did this, too. He walked through this world looking for those who would hear Him say, "Come, follow Me," and then actually get up and do it.

God calls us to an active response to Him, to a relationship of love and obedience in freedom. He wants us to choose Him moment by moment, not just once. It isn't about riding down a religious train track, checking the boxes on your holy to-do list. Instead, it is waking up each morning to a heart-to-heart time with the One Who loves you best, knowing He is eager to be with you and that in Him is everything you need. It's taking His hand and leaping up the side of the mountain, breathless, wondering where He is going to take you next. ♡

Study: Isaiah 1:18; Psalm 18:33

## *A Heart to Hear*

JANUARY 15 - 21

## The Burden-Bearer

This week has been difficult. Once again, I found myself taking up those same old burdens and concerns. My Abba Father had to sit me down and set me straight. Here is what He had to say:

"You don't have to fix it. Back to Step 1 – What are you carrying? Did you think I wouldn't see it if you put it on your back? You have taken up loads you can't handle. They aren't for you to bear. I alone am Savior, Redeemer. Trust Me. Lay them down again at My feet and trust Me.

"Fear comes between us like a glass wall. You know I'm here, but you don't feel My presence, My grace, or My love. Don't allow fear to move in. Worry and anxiety not only rob your joy, they cause you to behave in ways that actually further the plans of the enemy. You must reject fear. Kick it out the door. It is not your friend. Choose to trust Me. I see you. I know your heart.

"Cry out to Me. Bring Me all your concerns, and then move into faith, speaking the truth about Who I Am over the ones you love and their lives. Praise Me. Focus your heart on Who I Am. Magnify Me, not the problem. Begin to thank Me for how I will glorify My Name

## A Heart to Hear

through the solutions that are already on the way.

"When you choose to live this way, you enter into the life of Heaven even while your body still lives on this earth. You open a channel for My power to flow through."

*Yes, Lord. Please give us grace to live this way. I love You, Abba, and I thank You for never being too busy to be my Daddy.* ♡

"Praise be to the Lord, to God our Savior, Who daily bears our burdens." —Psalm 68:19

# *A Heart to Hear*

### JANUARY 22 - 28
## Call To Be Single-minded

Yesterday morning, my mind was bombarded with a dozen different thoughts pulling me in as many different directions. I struggled just to pray through the Lord's Prayer, distracted by everything from the state of my carpet to the state of the world.

Then the Holy Spirit gently dropped a word into my mind: *single-mindedness*. I needed single-mindedness, the grace to focus on "the one thing that is needful." I like that word, *needful*. It means "necessary or essential."

Isn't it wonderful how the Word of God can come to mind long after you've heard it? This phrase, "the one thing that is needful," must have bubbled up in the King James from my childhood memory. It is from a conversation Jesus had with Martha when she came to Him to complain about having to do all the work while her sister Mary sat at His feet. Jesus heard her out, and then He gently told her, "Martha, Martha, you are worried and troubled about many things. But one thing is needed, and Mary has chosen that good part, which will not be taken away from her."

Jesus was telling Martha that the best use of her time at that moment was to sit down with Him. He didn't want her running around trying to anticipate His needs and rushing

## A Heart to Hear

ahead to meet them. He wanted to meet her needs. He wanted her to be refreshed and restored by listening to His words that He had for her.

There will always be too many things that need to be done. Before we plunge into action, we need to stop and listen to the Voice that speaks with the perspective of eternity. Jesus faced tremendous demands from those around Him, but He took the time to get alone and listen to the voice of His Abba Father. He knew that it was the one thing that is needful.

It is often the hardest thing in the world, dragging my eyes off my to-do list and getting quiet before Him, but it is always, always worth it. He alone has the words of life, and it is His delight to speak them to a listening heart.

*Lord, please give us a heart to hear You.* ♡

Study: Luke 10:41-4; 2 John 6:68

## *A Heart to Hear*

JANUARY 29 - FEBRUARY 4

# Find Your Place and Fill It

Yesterday, I thought I knew what to write about this week. After spending the morning working on it, however, I knew in my heart that it just wasn't a "now" word.

At that point, all I could do was ask, "Okay, Father, what do You want to say today?" What I heard was this: "Find your place and fill it!"

Now the beautiful thing about this word is that there is no condemnation in it at all. There is no need to be anxious or to worry that this is an impossible task. It is an encouragement. The mental image is not one of running around frantically looking for a place. Instead, it is more like standing still and recognizing the place you already occupy. It is about seeing who you are and where you fit.

Psalm 127:1 says that unless the Lord builds the house, they that build it labor in vain. First Peter 2:5 tells us that God is building us, as living stones, into a spiritual house.

The wonderful thing is that when God builds, He doesn't use bricks all formed from the same mold. No, He likes to use living stones, and as a Master Builder, He knows how to place each individual stone in order to bring beauty and strength to the wall.

God has put each one of us in our own unique place. This

## *A Heart to Hear*

is defined in part by who we relate to, where we live, where we work, and where we plug into the Body of Christ. It is also defined by who we are. We each have personalities, giftings, and life experiences that have shaped us into who we are. I can't fill your spot, and you can't fill mine. You alone are able to fully occupy the space with your name on it.

One of the enemy's favorite schemes is to prevent us from filling our place by keeping us isolated, running from authentic relationship. He also loves to keep us trying to fill someone else's place. We think, "If I can just be like that person, then I'll really be pleasing to God." No, you please God by being who He made you to be, not someone else.

Ask the Father to speak to you about your place. Ask Him what He has for you to do and who He wants your life to touch today. Rejoice! God has a role for each of us in His kingdom, a vital part that only we can play.

So, places everyone! It is time to begin! ♡

# *A Heart to Hear*

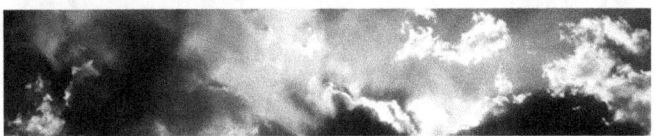

**FEBRUARY 5 - 11**

## Focus!

One of the enemy's favorite tricks is to keep me focused on what I don't have. How easy it is for me to get swept away by the latest catalog in the mail. Suddenly, I'm mentally redecorating the entire house.

It can also happen to me at church. I hear a wonderful message about God's plan for our lives, and it isn't long before I'm bubbling with plans for giving my family a spiritual extreme makeover!

Needless to say, this is not where my heart needs to be. My Heavenly Father wants me focused on Him, and on the life He has given me. This means living in the present moment and receiving it as a gift from Him. My circumstances have been allowed by a loving Father. Some of them may be the result of my choices. Some of them may be completely beyond my control. But all of them can be used to draw me nearer to Him.

For years, I grieved over the fact that my mother was far away and couldn't come over to spend time with my babies or go shopping with me. All I could see was what I didn't have. I wish that I had opened my heart to the possibility that God had someone right in front of me who could step into that place and be an adopted mom to me.

## A Heart to Hear

Just as the Holy Spirit gives us the spirit of adoption that enables us to know we are God's chosen children, I believe He also gives us grace to adopt each other. I was so blessed last Sunday watching Cindy, a friend at church, love on her adopted daughter and granddaughters. The joy was contagious!

Jesus said the kingdom of Heaven is at hand. Let's ask the Lord to open our eyes to see what He has put at our fingertips. Let's ask Him for the wisdom and grace to love the ones He has placed within our arm's reach. It could be as simple as making a phone call or taking the time to say, "How are you doing?" and listening to the answer with an open heart.

Today is a precious gift. It is the place where God's grace flows. It is where we see His kingdom come and His will get done in and through us! ♡

"You will keep in perfect peace all who trust in you, all whose thoughts are fixed on you!" —Isaiah 26:2-4 (NLT)

## *A Heart to Hear*

**FEBRUARY 12 - 18**

# Blindsided!

Have you ever been blindsided by the enemy? Utterly thrown off your groove by something you never saw coming?

That happened to me this week. I was moving along pretty steadily when out of the pit came a new challenger to test my heart. Do I really believe what I say? Will I keep my focus on "The One Thing" when I've taken a crushing blow?

Here's the worst part: It was an inside job. Not only did the blow come through someone I trusted, it hit the perfect target—my own insecurity. Talk about your one-two punches. I was down for the count, ready to crawl into a hole and pull it in after me.

Ever been there? It's the place where it's hard to even think about crying out to God. Why is He letting this happen?

Psalm 13 captures this place really well, especially verse 2. It says in the NIV: "How long must I wrestle with my thoughts and every day have sorrow in my heart? How long will my enemy triumph over me?"

I've been wrestling with my thoughts, but, thankfully, today my Abba Father was able to slip in a few of His own. I seem to hear the Lord very clearly in the place between sleeping and waking. This morning, I remembered hearing Beth Moore on "Life Today" talking about Hebrews 10:35, which

## *A Heart to Hear*

says, "Therefore, do not throw away your confidence, which has a great reward." As she discussed the enemy's plans to destroy our confidence, she spoke of how often it is those we trust who are most effective at causing us to doubt what God has said. She spoke of the need to discern when a loved one may not be speaking truth to us and the challenge of continuing to love even when we cannot accept their input.

You know it must have been God for all that to come bubbling up while I'm still half asleep!

Then I saw the situation from God's perspective: He had given me the truth and the warning, but I still stepped into the enemy's snare. Why? Because my own insecurity made me totally vulnerable to something that really wasn't worth a second thought, much less days of wrestling. *Oy!* Yet, even here, I see mercy because my Abba Father knew I had a weak place that needed His touch, and the only way I would find out was by getting hit there.

Pastor said on Sunday that evil is our enemy, not people. For a while, I thought my friend was the enemy and the source of my pain. No, my enemy is the evil one who seeks to triumph over me and get me to throw away my confidence in who God has made me. Thanks be to God, He gets the victory by using what the enemy meant to crush me as a means to bring wholeness to yet another part of my heart. David must have seen this, too, because he finished up Psalm 13 like this: "But I trust in Your unfailing love; my heart rejoices in Your salvation. I will sing to the Lord, for he has been good to me."

Yes, and Amen. It's time to go sing! ♡

## *A Heart to Hear*

**FEBRUARY 19 - 25**

# Draw Near!

Sunday morning at church, we experienced the presence of the Lord in a wonderful way. It was one of those times when we get a little taste of what Heaven must be like when everyone comes together to worship the Lord. Adoration, praise, and thanksgiving flowed out of our hearts, and greater awareness of God's love for us flowed in. It was awesome, and I almost wished it never had to end.

Now, Monday morning is here in all its glory—morning routines, breakfast dishes, neglected laundry, looming bills, and all the rest. I'm pondering how to bridge the gap between these two realities.

The key is His presence. Psalm 139 makes it clear that there is nowhere to go to escape God's presence. He is everywhere. Yet, many times, the Bible speaks of entering His presence. Hebrews 10:22 encourages us to draw near to God in full assurance of faith. Jesus told us to abide in Him, for apart from Him we can do nothing (Jn. 15:5). *Abide* simply means "stay." Jesus would not have told us we needed to do this unless we were going to have to make an effort to make it happen. Entering into His presence is something we must learn to do.

As great as Sunday was, it wasn't enough to get me

## *A Heart to Hear*

through the week. This morning, when I woke up to life and all its challenges, I needed to get into the presence of the Lord. The best way I know to do this is found in Psalm 100:4-5:

> "Enter into His gates with thanksgiving, and into His courts with praise. Be thankful to Him, and bless His name. For the LORD is good; His mercy is everlasting, and His truth endures to all generations."

For me today, this looked like going in my room and putting worship music on my MP3 player and my focus on the Lord. Worship is one of those things that is easier in private. Coming together to worship is vital, but it makes a huge difference if you've been doing it on your own. Worship is the door to God's presence: bowing down before Him, remembering that the blood of Jesus opened the door, reveling in His great mercy, experiencing forgiveness, realizing He's my Shepherd, and He will take care of me.

Wow! How can I not cry out praise and thankfulness to Him? He is good! When I take time to see Him and to see how good He is, it changes my entire outlook. Suddenly, that gap between Sunday and Monday just got closed. This is how life is meant to be lived. It won't always be a celebration. Sometimes it will be a brief respite from a raging battle. But knowing God is with us is something we can't afford to be without.

I love sharing what I hear the Lord saying, but don't neglect asking the Lord to speak His words of life to you. Enter His presence and listen! ♡

## *A Heart to Hear*

**FEBRUARY 26 - MARCH 4**

# Hold On To Your Hope

Hold on to your hope! That is the word for today. It may be dark, but the morning is coming. It may be raining, but the sun will shine again. It may be cold and gray, but spring is on its way.

These may sound like clichés, but they are actually examples of the many ways God has woven the reality of hope into the fiber of our beings. Just as surely as you don't doubt that summer in Texas will be hot, don't doubt that our God is faithful. He will do what He has promised. He alone is faithful.

Life is hard. My husband heard the Lord speak to him recently that it is okay that it is hard. It isn't necessarily because you are doing something wrong. Life is hard period. As long as we are living in a world where people are free to choose God or not, life will be hard. I don't know what you are facing today, but I am certain that all of us are facing some really tough situations.

I love reading the psalms of David because he had a real relationship with God even while living through very difficult circumstances. In Psalm 62, he describes himself as a leaning wall or a tottering fence, constantly under attack. Still, he tells himself:

## A Heart to Hear

"Find rest, O my soul, in God alone; my hope comes from Him. He alone is my rock and my salvation; He is my fortress, I will not be shaken. My salvation and my honor depend on God; He is my mighty rock, my refuge. Trust in Him at all times, O people; pour out your hearts to Him, for God is our refuge."

Enough said. Hold on to your hope, and don't let go! He who has promised is faithful. ♡

Study: Romans 15:13; Romans 16:20; Philippians 4:4-7

# *A Heart to Hear*

### MARCH 5 - 11
## Who Are You Wearing

Who are you wearing? That's the question all the actresses are asked on the red carpet. Everyone wants to know who deserves the credit or, in some cases, the blame.

Who are you wearing? That question has been echoing in my thoughts lately. As I waited before the Lord, He held up His mirror and let me see what and who I was wearing.

The first thing I saw was a dense, black cloak sitting heavily on my shoulders and making it hard to do anything with my hands—it was a spirit of heaviness and hopelessness. Then I noticed a thick, choking scarf full of knots wrapped around my neck—it was fear trying to choke the life out of me. On my feet were high-heeled shoes that made me wobble and pinch my toes—I was trying to live up to what I imagined was expected of me. On my head was a band of guilt squeezing my brain and never letting me relax.

Who do you suppose is the designer of this ensemble? Of course, it is custom made by the enemy who loves nothing better than to torture and torment.

The question I am asking myself now is why would I choose to dress this way? I know Isaiah 61:3 declares that God's design for me is a garment of praise instead of a spirit of despair. I know that perfect love casts out fear. God has

## *A Heart to Hear*

promised that He will instruct me and teach me His ways. I know that the blood of Jesus cleanses me from all my sin. I know that my heavenly Father will complete the work He has started in me. I know that nothing can separate me from His love. So why am I standing here looking like a candidate for "What Not to Wear - Holy Spirit Edition"?

It is simply because I haven't been actively choosing to live by the Spirit. I have defaulted to my original programming of living according to the desires of my flesh: choosing extra sleep over time spent seeking the Lord before the day begins, attempting to run on the empty tank of my own sufficiency.

In Romans 13:14, the apostle Paul tells us to "put on the Lord Jesus Christ and make no provision for the flesh in regard to its lusts." The flesh desires above all else to find a way to function apart from relationship with God, but the end result is always hopelessness and despair. Just as standing on three-inch stilettos doesn't really make me taller, all of my human attempts to be good are doomed to fail. I have to choose each day, each hour, sometimes each moment to put on the Lord Jesus Christ. To put on Jesus is to admit that my only hope for a life worth living is found in Him.

Galatians 5:1 tells us, "It is for freedom that Christ has set us free. Stand firm, then, and do not let yourselves be burdened again by a yoke of slavery."

To be passive is to be a prisoner. Let's choose freedom in Christ, even when it is a battle to believe and walk in the truth. ♡

## *A Heart to Hear*

**MARCH 12 - 18**

## Blank Check

"We have this treasure in jars of clay to show that this all-surpassing power is from God and not from us."
—2 Corinthians 4:7

You know that special little tingle you get when you head out shopping and you've got some money in your purse that's just for you to spend? We ought to feel that way every day!

Our Abba Father has given us a blank check! He said:

> "Ask Me and just see what I will do. Seek me and you won't believe the treasure you will find. Knock and you are going to be blown away by the doors I will open."

That's Matthew 7:7-8, my own translation. It's not about piling up a bunch of blessings for ourselves, so we can settle down and be comfortable. It's about knowing we have the power to bring God's kingdom to earth every single day. Through the prayers we pray, through the words we say, through the people God tells us to reach out to. We need to get in the habit of looking for the way God wants to use us each day. Jesus is the treasure inside of us, His Spirit fills us, and we have the mind of Christ. We don't have to wonder,

## A Heart to Hear

"What would Jesus do?" We can ask Him what He wants to do. He's here!

*Father, help us understand what we really have inside of us. Help us pull away to the quiet place where we can hear You speak. Help us hear, and give us grace to believe what You say. Enable us to do the things that seem hard. Thank You for being all we need. In Jesus' name. Amen.* ♡

## *A Heart to Hear*

**MARCH 19 - 25**
## Believing Is The Key

There is a beautiful old book called *The Secret Garden* that tells the story of an unloved orphan girl named Mary who discovers a garden locked behind high walls. She eventually finds the key, and experiences a personal transformation as she works to restore the garden to its original glory.

This story is the backdrop for the word the Lord spoke to me this week: *Believing is the key that unlocks the door to the garden.*

As long as I engage my mind in worrying, doubting, and fearing, I wander alone on desolate pathways. When I choose to believe what God has said, I am able to open the door to the garden of His presence. This is the place of peace, trust, and victory. On the outside, I am miserable and lonely. Inside, my heart is warmed by the light of God's love shining down on me. I remember His promises, and I plant them as seeds, knowing that they are going to bloom gloriously because my Abba Father says so.

This garden isn't any small place either. As I explore, I find the path to the promised land, the place God has set aside for me to claim in the name of His Son. He teaches me to battle the enemy for possession and how to clear the land and plant it for a harvest. But none of it will ever happen if I don't take

## *A Heart to Hear*

the key and unlock the door by believing what God says.

1 Thessalonians 2:13 tells us that those who receive the Word of God and believe it experience His mighty, effective power at work in them! It is a two-step process: receive God's Word, and believe God's Word. This means we've got to dig into the Word, to really know what it says. Then, we must believe. This is not mere passive acceptance. Believing means to adhere to, trust in, rely on, and entrust oneself to it.

Think of bungee jumping. We will only take that leap if we believe the equipment will hold us. That is the degree to which God wants us believing Him and His Word.

When we trust in Him and no other, that is when we will see His power at work in our lives and receive His peace, His provision, His grace to faithfully tend the land He has put in our care. Believe that He who has promised is faithful. Turn the key. Enter into His presence, and live in His power and love. ♡

## *A Heart to Hear*

MARCH 26 - APRIL 1
## Go With What You Know!

Our pastor preached last Sunday on living in a way that changes our world by bringing the Kingdom of God to the places where we live. It was a great message, and my heart was saying, "Yes, Lord, show me where to start!"

I have always wanted to have a significant impact on this planet. In second grade, I had a "Ziggy" pencil bag that was printed on the side with, "Things to make my mark on the world!" I took that seriously. I really wanted the world to be different because I had been here.

I believe this is something God puts in every human heart. The impulse may get buried, but deep down, we all want to know that our lives matter. I don't know about you, but as soon as my mind gets hold of this idea, it starts charging down the track like a runaway train, trying to figure out how in the world I am going to make it happen. Major upheaval, grand ventures, and heart-wrenching sacrifices all flash across my mental movie screen as I imagine what God will have me do.

However, by the time I've gone home, made lunch, and cleaned the kitchen, I'm more concerned with making sure everyone has clean jeans for Monday than bringing the Kingdom to earth.

This morning, however, the Lord brought Sunday's sermon

## A Heart to Hear

back to my attention, and He spoke some things to my heart that gave me a new perspective. I was musing over a verse I found last week that really intrigued me. It is Philippians 3:16. It's a quiet, obscure little verse that gets overshadowed by the passage that precedes it where Paul makes his stirring statement about pressing on toward the goal to win the prize for which God called him. Here it is: "Only let us live up to what we have already attained."

How hard that can be! Too often, it is so tempting to slack off and go back to the old ruts we ran in before God's grace pulled us out. The enemy lies to us and says, "You know, you really need a break. Just let this slide." Before we know it, we've slidden a whole lot farther than we planned.

God paraphrased this verse for me today like this: "Go with what you know! Those truths you have learned, many of them the hard way, live them!" Then He tied it back in to the idea of making an impact where I live. I could hear Him saying, "Jennifer, you don't need to run around looking for a place to make a difference. Work with what you've got!" He began to remind me of the people with whom He has given me relationship, and how I've blown past them mentally as I made my grand plans to serve the Kingdom. What if His call to me is to love the people He has already brought into my life? What if He has already given me all the opportunities I can handle, and I just haven't seen them because they didn't look like I thought they would?

Go with what you know. Work with what you've got. See the Kingdom come. Yes! ♡

# *A Heart to Hear*

### APRIL 2 - 8

## Pouring Water On Dry Ground

Have you ever watched a young child who has just received a wonderful gift? The little face is all lit up with joy and anticipation.

What happens next? Usually, the child jumps up to go play with the new acquisition, completely forgetting the giver. "What do you say?" prompts mom or dad. "Thank you," the little one chirps, in a hurry, but aware that this is the required response.

Parents have to work hard from an early age to instill in their children the message that expressing gratitude is important. We certainly don't want our children to grow up with the idea that they are entitled to every good thing and have no need to look beyond their blessings to the source.

The ability to feel and express gratitude is one of the foundation stones of love. Expressing thankfulness and appreciation is like pouring water on the dry ground of our relationships. Conversely, taking those who love us for granted can cause the ground to harden and the plant to wither.

Over and over in God's Word, we find the command to give thanks to the Lord. Our Father God wants us to walk through this life with an awareness of Him and His goodness to us. Psalm 95:2 tells us that giving thanks ushers us into

## *A Heart to Hear*

God's presence. The Apostle Paul tells us to give thanks as we make our requests to God (Phil. 4:6).

Being thankful to God is a hallmark of a living relationship with Him. It shows that we look past the many incredible blessings He pours out upon us to see Him and to express our love and appreciation for Him. When we express our thanks to the Lord, it doesn't just bless His heart, but ours as well. We are reconnected once again to the truth that apart from Him, we have nothing. We are reminded that our call is to seek His face, not just His hand. To be grateful is a gift. It is a wake-up call to our hearts to open our eyes to all the ways His kindness and love is being poured out upon us. ♡

"Give thanks to the Lord, for He is good; His love endures forever." —1 Chronicles 16:34

# *A Heart to Hear*

### APRIL 9 - 15
## Don't Let Your Mind Wander

Ever hear the old joke, "Don't let your mind wander; it's too little to go out alone!"? It's funny, but there is a kernel of truth in it. When I let my mind go off-road, away from the love of my Abba Father, it isn't long before I'm up to my axles in muck.

The Apostle Paul put it this way: "The mind set on the flesh is death, but the mind set on the Spirit is life and peace" (Ro. 8:6). What does it mean to set your mind on the flesh? Well, it might mean obsessing about a relationship, or worrying constantly about your weight, or lying awake nights fearfully reviewing your finances. Essentially it is setting your mind on what flesh can do, instead of centering it on what God alone can do. The result is clear—life or death.

My family can always tell when my mind is set on the flesh. They may not know what to call it, but they know it isn't pretty. This is why it is so important to be aware of the traffic in our heads. Many thoughts can be rushing through our minds, like one of those freeway intersections with bridges and ramps going in every direction. It is very easy to get on the wrong road. The next thing you know, you're heading in the opposite direction of where you wanted to go, and finding a spot to turn around always takes longer than you want it to.

## A Heart to Hear

Books, movies, TV shows, songs on the radio, internet news—we are flooded with input daily. The enemy is also actively throwing in his rogue thoughts, trying to trick us into adopting them as our own. For example, last week I picked up a book from the library, just a little light fiction about a group of friends who make quilts. It took me a few days to clue in to the fact that a negative attitude toward men was taking root in my brain. The thoughts and feelings of one of the characters was having a negative influence on me.

Here's another example of taking a mental wrong turn: Someone at church brushes past us without speaking. Immediately we go into mental overdrive wondering what we could have done to offend them. Before we are through, we feel offended right back at them! The enemy loves this one. After much wasted worry, it usually turns out the other person's mind was having its own off-road adventure that had absolutely nothing to do with us.

This is why I love the Word of God; it is the solid road under my wheels. Galatians 6:8 says, "For the one who sows to his own flesh will of the flesh reap corruption, but the one who sows to the Spirit will from the Spirit reap eternal life." This takes us right back to that fork in the road. Will we choose life or death? Will we focus our thoughts on a perfect Father in Heaven who has it all under control, even when things feel out of control? Will we let Him be our Guide each step of the way? There may be some rugged roads ahead, but He has promised to never leave us, and to perfect those things that concern us. When we choose to rest in that truth, we begin to walk in the eternal life that is meant to be ours right now. ♡

## *A Heart to Hear*

**APRIL 16 - 22**

# Change Is Inescapable

Change is inescapable. Nothing stays the same for long in this world. That's the heartbreaking thing about housework, isn't it? You can get it all clean, but it surely isn't going to stay that way!

From beginning to end, our lives are constantly changing in every way possible. Our bodies change, our circumstances change, people around us change, and we change. We change our minds, change our addresses, change our clothes, and change our hair color! Every morning when we turn on our computers, we check to see what has changed since we went to bed the night before. Sometimes all the changes become overwhelming.

Have you ever gone back to visit a town where you lived years ago, only to find that things are so different you can't find your way around? In your mind, the place was still the same, but in your absence the place had the audacity to change!

I grew up in a family that moved around a good bit. My grandmother's house was the one place that was a constant for me. I will never forget how sad I was when she remodeled her kitchen and got a new back door. I had always loved the sound her old door made as it closed. This was one of my first hints

## *A Heart to Hear*

that nothing ever stays the same, not even Grandma's house.

In a world where nothing stays the same, our hearts cry out for something that never changes, a rock that never moves.

When I asked the Lord what He had to say to us this week, this is what I heard: *I never change.*

He is our Rock in the sea of change around us. He is the One who is faithful and true. James calls Him the Father of the heavenly lights who does not change like shifting shadows.

Hebrews 13:8 tells us that Jesus is the same yesterday, today, and forever. Hebrews 1:12 says that the heavens themselves will be rolled up like a garment and changed, but the One who made them does not change. He is the God of peace. His mercy is new every morning. His faithfulness reaches to the highest height, and His love is deeper and wider than the biggest ocean. He is the One who redeems the lost, heals the broken hearted, and sets the captives free. He never lies, he never forgets us, and His purposes are never thwarted.

He is our Shepherd, our Provider, our Comforter, and our soon-coming King. This is our God, and …

He Never Changes! ♡

## *A Heart to Hear*

### APRIL 23 - 29
## False Perception

What you don't know can't hurt you. Ever heard that one? Unfortunately, it just isn't true. What you don't know can hurt you tremendously. What I believe about life affects all of my responses to it. If what I believe is wrong, my responses will be wrong, too.

This is especially true in the area of relationships. It is so easy to assume that we know the reasons people in our lives behave the way they do, but usually we have no idea what is really going on in their hearts.

One night a long time ago, we were eating dinner at Pancho's with our daughter, Catherine, who was about a year old at the time. She was sitting in the highchair, and I was giving her little bits of food. All of a sudden, I became convinced she was choking. The restaurant was noisy, and I couldn't hear if she was breathing or not. Being the rookie mom that I was, I panicked. I flipped the tray up and over, sending a plastic box of wipes flying across the room. Then I snatched my baby up out of the chair and smacked her on the leg, causing her to cry. I'm sure anyone watching thought I was a crazy person, but I was desperate to know if she was able to breathe, and that was the first thing that came to mind.

My point is this: judging my actions would have given no clue as to the true motivation of my heart. How many times have I judged someone else's actions or words without knowing the truth?

## *A Heart to Hear*

Our Abba Father wants us to know and walk in the truth. Jesus said, "You will know the truth and the truth will set you free" (Jn. 8:32). The Lord spoke this to me: *So much of what hurts us isn't real. It is a false perception of reality.* Then He showed me that something I had grieved over for years was based on an assumption about someone else's motives that was not accurate. The enemy had gleefully tormented me with a lie, and my belief had caused me to behave in conflict and bitterness. Over and over, I tried to get past the pain and resentment. In fact, I was struggling with forgiveness yet again when the Lord spoke this truth to me.

So much of what hurts us isn't real. It is a false perception of reality. Suddenly, I saw that my belief about how that person felt was wrong. It was a skewed view of reality. As quickly as I saw it for a lie, the hurt was gone, and I was free to forgive. Amazing! Truth really does set us free! Lies we believe about ourselves, other people or even God become chains that bind us to wrong ways of thinking and wrong ways of responding.

Even when you have a heart to follow the Lord and walk in His ways, if you are believing a lie, you won't be able to walk in the freedom He has for you. The enemy loves to distort our perceptions of reality. Insecurity, past hurts, and unforgiveness are just a few of the things that can warp our vision and cause us to suffer.

Let's ask the Lord to show us where we have believed lies about others or even about Him. Look for the places that are causing you the most pain. That is usually a good indicator that something is out of alignment with the truth. With the truth comes freedom, and with freedom comes joy. This is our Abba Father's desire for us—freedom with joy. Don't settle for anything less! ♡

# *A Heart to Hear*

**APRIL 30 - MAY 6**

## Fight for Your Freedom

Tied up, tied down, held back, stuck, imprisoned, trapped, captive; these are all words that describe lack of freedom. These are also words that describe exactly where the enemy wants to keep us. What I hear the Lord saying this week is: *Fight for your freedom!*

Galatians 5:1 tells us, "It is for freedom that Christ has set us free. Stand firm, then, and do not let yourselves be burdened again by a yoke of slavery." Jesus told us He came to proclaim freedom for the captives and release from darkness for the prisoners (Is. 61, Lk. 4:18-20). That means us! We are meant to walk in freedom! It brings glory and honor to the name of Jesus when we do.

Our Abba Father sent Jesus to free us from bondage to sin, fear, and death. To choose a life of captivity when my prison door has been opened is a tragedy; yet, so many times I do just that. I know I'm called to live in relationship with other people, but sometimes, there is a temptation to hide out in my comfy little hobbit hole and refuse to come out. All too quickly my pleasant escape becomes a prison. I need to be involved with the people God has brought into my life, for their sake and for mine.

We all have our battlegrounds, places where the enemy

## *A Heart to Hear*

lies to us and invites us to take refuge in his houses of straw. Freedom means knowing that God is our refuge, and He is with us wherever He sends us, whether it's across the street or across an ocean.

For years I feared going overseas because I was afraid something would happen, and I wouldn't be able to get home. When God asked me to go to China, He broke that fear, and the whole world opened up for me. Don't let the enemy lock you up in a box!

Right now, I am battling for freedom in the area of my household spending. I'm not there yet, but I have at least begun to realize that the frustration and sense of failure I consistently experience in this area is not the freedom God has for me. I am listening for the truth, and turning over rocks looking for the lies that have kept me stuck in the same place for way too long. My hope is not in my ability to figure it out, but in my Abba Father who wants me to be free even more than I do. He wants the same thing for you.

Where do you feel stuck, trapped, or unable to move? That is the place where you need to start fighting for your freedom! ♡

## *A Heart to Hear*

MAY 7 - 13

# Relax and Enjoy the Ride

Are you one of those crazy people who likes to ride roller coasters? For my money, there are lots more fun things to do than being plunged down a huge drop and then twisted and turned within an inch of my life at maximum velocity. I have such a deep aversion to these large-scale instruments of torture that they occasionally pop up in my dreams.

For me, the worst part is the drop. The slow climb to the top is an agonizing wait for the moment of terror when it feels as if the bottom has dropped out of the world. I hate the drops! I always want to grab hold of something, anything, rather than experience that plunge.

I was dreaming about this very scenario the other night. I was trying to hold on, but then I realized my fingers were going to get hurt if I didn't let go. I realized that I needed to relax and go with it because it was going to be over soon anyway.

The next morning I was thinking it over, and I felt like God was speaking to me in this dream. Life has a lot of similarities to a roller coaster, doesn't it? You have highs and lows, twists and turns, and sometimes you feel like you won't make it unless you scream your head off.

We all have areas where we are waiting on God to move, waiting for His provision to come, waiting for His promises

## *A Heart to Hear*

to be fulfilled. Those deadlines are looming, and we start getting anxious. Will the money come in time? Will the healing happen? Will the relationship get restored before it is too late?

We start trying to figure out how to make sure everything is going to turn out like we think it should. We start putting a death grip on the people or things around us, trying to hold on before it all gets beyond our grasp.

What I hear our Abba Father saying is this:

*Relax and enjoy the ride! Trust Me to be all you need. Even if you go over the edge, I won't let you fall too far. My hand is holding on to you, even when you can't find the strength to hold on to Me. Don't worry about all the ups and downs, twists and turns. They are part of the journey. Just trust Me. I am going to make sure you get to the place I have for you. I have promised to meet all your needs. I am your All-Sufficient One. Yell if you need to, but know that you are safe in My arms always. Relax and enjoy the ride.* ♡

"Be strong and courageous. Do not be afraid or terrified … for the LORD your God goes with you; He will never leave you nor forsake you." —Deuteronomy 31:6

## A Heart to Hear

**MAY 14 - 20**

# Stand Still!

There are times when the only thing God wants from us is stillness. Have you ever struggled to calm a child in distress and known the wonder in that moment when the child is finally still, just resting her head on your shoulder? You feel the weight of the little body settling down and resting in your arms, fully trusting the security of your embrace. You breathe in the peace, so thankful for this moment of rest.

Our Abba Father longs for those moments with us. He desires rest for our souls. He wants us to get to that place where we aren't doing anything except resting in His arms, completely trusting the safety of His embrace.

For most of us, springing into action is way more comfortable than waiting on God. Sunday morning, I woke to the sounds of my little girls in the kitchen, getting themselves a bowl of cereal. As I heard the cabinet door slam, I remembered that I had stuffed three big bottles of soda onto the top shelf of the fridge to chill for our picnic at the lake. They were going to have a major problem when they tried to get the milk down!

I jumped out of bed, and raced downstairs only to find they had gotten to the milk just fine. I then proceeded to put everything back and somehow managed to drop the nearly

## A Heart to Hear

full jug of milk from the top shelf of the fridge, creating an explosion of milk that saturated my hair, my robe, the rug, and coated the inside of the fridge. Glory! No, actually that wasn't my first thought.

As I set about undoing the enormous mess I had created, I kept thinking that if I had just stayed in bed, everything would have been fine. My leap into action had caused my imagined, worst-case scenario to become a reality.

As I started the washing machine, I could hear the still, small voice of the Lord talking to my heart, encouraging me to learn from what had just happened. I needed to know that leaping into action apart from His Holy Spirit's leading only causes a bigger problem than the one I'm trying to fix.

I knew He was talking about things much more critical than spilled milk. Sometimes we face issues that require us to wait on the Lord. There were many times when the Lord sent the Israelites out to fight their enemies head-on, but there were also times when He said, "Stand still and see what I am going to do for you."

That is where I am today: waiting on the Lord to do what only He can do and trusting Him for the outcome. Choosing to rest in Him is a battle in itself. By an act of my will, I have laid all my burdens at His feet, and now I am choosing to rest my head on His shoulder and listen quietly to His heartbeat. He is my Abba Father, and He is all I need. ♡

"But I have stilled and quieted my soul; like a weaned child with its mother … is my soul within me … put your hope in the LORD both now and forevermore." —Psalm 131:2-3

# *A Heart to Hear*

MAY 21 - 27

## Keep Pressing In

The voice of the Lord is still and small. You can't hear it in the whirlwind. It's hard to hear it in the clamor of many voices. Those of you who know I have six children are probably thinking, *No kidding!* But I'm not just talking about the noise made by the people around me.

I have to pursue the stillness, not only of my outer environment, but also of my own heart. You wouldn't believe the racket my own mind is capable of producing.

Just as difficult to silence is the voice that says I have too much to do to take the time to get still. As if all that isn't enough, I also have to get past the whispering voice of the enemy in my ear, sometimes so close I think it is my own.

In a way, the design of the Temple is a picture of how we have to keep pressing in—through the outer court, the inner court, and the Holy Place until we finally get to the Holy of Holies where God's presence dwells. We have to push on past all the distractions in order to get to the place where we can quiet our hearts before the Lord and hear what He has to say to us. Is it worth it? Yes! Yes! A million times, yes!

Consider the alternative as voiced so clearly by David in Psalm 55:2-5, "My thoughts trouble me and I am distraught at the voice of the enemy ... My heart is in anguish within

## A Heart to Hear

me; the terrors of death assail me. Fear and trembling have beset me ..."

Anybody been there lately? I know I have. If I don't make the effort to enter in to God's presence to seek His face and hear His voice, I leave myself open to all the other voices filling up the space in and around me.

The problem is none of those voices speak what I really need to hear. As Peter told Jesus, "Lord, to whom shall we go? You have the words of eternal life" (Jn. 6:68). That is what I need more than anything in this world: the words of LIFE! That is who Jesus is and what He wants to give us. He is the Way, the Truth, and the Life that came to give us Life, now and forevermore.

Be tenacious! Go after His presence and His words of life as if they were the key to your survival because they are! I keep thinking of the woman who pressed through the crowd just to touch the edge of Jesus' robe because she knew He was her only hope.

Let your need drive you to be persistent. Don't stop pressing in until you reach Him. He is what we need! ♡

## *A Heart to Hear*

**MAY 28 - JUNE 3**

# I Don't Need Your Help!

*I don't need your help.* That is what I hear the Lord saying this week. Are you surprised? I'll bet you weren't expecting that one. Neither was I the first time I heard it.

Growing up, I went to church every time the doors were open. Actually, my dad had the keys, and sometimes we went when the doors weren't open. I was on the receiving end of countless sermons and Sunday school lessons, and they all seemed to be aimed at teaching me to do the things God wanted me to do. When I took on the roles of wife and mother, I saw myself partnering with God to raise godly children, not to mention a godly husband! Somehow though, I never seemed to be able to get my family to line up with my ideal.

One day, while reading Proverbs 14:1, I felt the Holy Spirit's laser sight hit me right between the eyes. "The wise woman builds her house, but with her own hands, the foolish one tears hers down." It was painful when God began to show me that my efforts to help Him do His work in the lives of those closest to me were actually hurting instead of helping. In my clueless pride, I thought I could help God make our family holy and right, but all of my efforts were doomed to fail, or as my kids would say, "epic fail."

James 1:20 (KJV) says, "For the wrath of man worketh not

## A Heart to Hear

the righteousness of God." I could paraphrase that to say, "A woman on the warpath will not bring about the life of God in her family." Verse 19 tells us to be "… quick to listen, slow to speak and slow to become angry." The opposite was more often true of me. I thought if I just tried hard enough, I could be the perfect mother and wife, and have the perfect godly family. I had to hit the wall of my own shortcomings many times before I was able to see that these wonderful goals weren't even godly. The people I love have wills of their own, and as a wise friend explained to me, you cannot make goals that violate another person's free will, as it leads to manipulation and frustration. I have to trust God to draw each one to Himself in His way and in His time. As for trying to be perfect, I finally had to accept that He designed me to need Him, and apart from Him, I really can do nothing (Jn. 15:5).

I am learning these truths only through the grace of God. He is teaching me to walk in humility. I'm learning to listen for His voice and rest in the knowledge that He doesn't need my help. I do have a role to play, but now I know that I'm not the director. My job is to love, to teach—more by example than words—to train, to pray, and most of all, to trust in the One who alone can save. The same God who has relentlessly pursued me is also pursuing the ones I love. I'll leave you with some words the Lord spoke to me recently in worship:

*I will accomplish My will. You put far too much emphasis and importance on your works. It's really just about your heart being Mine. You don't make My work happen. Rest in Me. It is My amazing grace. That is all.*

Thank You, Abba Father! ♡

# *A Heart to Hear*

### JUNE 4 - 10
# He's Got Your Back

What do an electric hedge trimmer, one silver earring, and a set of car keys have in common? They were all used by God this week to speak to my heart.

Last week, I wrote about how God doesn't need my help to achieve His purposes in my family. Unfortunately, the same day that word came to you, I found myself right back in the battle to believe that truth. Surely a few well-spoken words in the right ear could turn things around. A carefully reasoned argument was sure to change a heart and bring transformation.

That might work in a *Lifetime* movie but definitely not at my house! Clearly, I needed a refresher course in trust.

My first lesson came when I was trimming the bushes around my house and caught my finger with the trimmer. I still have no explanation for how I managed to hit my finger with a running power tool and only get a small cut. Once I stopped shaking, I started thanking the Lord for saving my finger.

Lesson two came next. I was leaving the elementary school where I had attended a program for one of my children. I was parked on the hill next to the school because the lot had been full when I arrived. As I walked up to my car, I was stunned to see my car keys lying on the ground in front of my car! In my rush to make it to the program on time,

## *A Heart to Hear*

I guess I threw my keys at my purse and missed. Again, all I could do was thank the Lord that my car was still there.

Next, I headed to the mall to look for a new pair of earrings. While I was shopping, I took off the earring I was wearing and hung it on the edge of my shopping bag. I wanted it out of the way while I held up possible choices to my ear. Intent on finding just the right pair, I completely forgot about my favorite French wire earring dangling on the edge of the bag until I got back to my car and it fell off onto the console. Unbelievable!

Now, some of you are probably thinking, *Where is this woman's brain?* That is a good question! However, as I sat in my car and gratefully put my pretty earring back in, I realized all over again that God really is able to take care of me. Even when I'm screwing up all over the place, He's got my back! My Abba Father is so good. I truly can trust Him with everything! Sometimes the battle to believe it is fierce, but it's always worth it. ♡

"Surely God is my salvation; I will trust and not be afraid. The LORD, the LORD, is my strength and my song; He has become my salvation." —Isaiah 12:2

## *A Heart to Hear*

JUNE 11 - 17

# Going On Vacation

This week I've been on vacation! What a blessing it was to have the opportunity to step back from my daily routine for a few days.

One of the most fun things I got to do on my trip was to go out riding trails on a four wheeler. At first, I was a little nervous because I hadn't done anything like that since I was a teenager, and it's nobody's business how long ago that was!

The most unnerving thing was when the trail dropped out of sight because it was so steep on the other side. I had to trust that the path would be there when I got there. Those parts of the trail did inspire a little high volume praying!

Later, when I was spending some time with the Lord, He spoke this to me:

*I know you, Jennifer. I know every step of your journey—all the ones you've already taken and all the ones you have yet to take. I have been with you every step of the way, and I will never leave you, never forsake you. I am Your God, and I AM ENOUGH!*

Yes, Lord! I don't know what is around the bend in the road. I only know that my Abba Father will be there.

## *A Heart to Hear*

Sometimes the path drops out of sight, but I know that others have gone before me and made it. I won't wimp out. I will choose to enjoy the ride, trust my Father, and have fun! ♡

"It was not by their sword that they won the land, nor did their arm bring them victory; it was Your right hand, Your arm, and the light of Your face, for you loved them." —Psalm 44:3

## *A Heart to Hear*

JUNE 18 - 24

## Heart On Overload

Have you ever found yourself dashing into the store for one or two things only to arrive at the checkout juggling two dozen assorted items? I've never seen a man doing this, but somehow, we women seem to believe we can always carry one more thing. I think we have a tendency to do this mentally and emotionally as well.

So many things are competing for our attention that oftentimes the end result is overwhelmed confusion. It's time to sit down and empty our mental pockets. Making lists and prioritizing them is helpful, but sometimes even that is not enough.

Our hearts are overloaded, too. We are carrying many concerns: decisions to be made, worries for loved ones, needs yet to be supplied, hurts that need to be comforted, offenses that haven't been resolved. We feel caught in a whirlwind, and our hearts are so heavy.

We need to stop and take the time to pour it all out before the Lord. David knew how to do this, and the Lord always met him in the place of honesty. Look at Psalm 142. David wrote this in a cave. (Don't we all wish we could find a cave to hide out in sometimes?)

## A Heart to Hear

"I cry aloud to the LORD; I lift up my voice to the LORD for mercy. I pour out my complaint before Him; before Him I tell my trouble. When my spirit grows faint within me, it is You who know my way ... I cry to you, O LORD; I say, "You are my refuge, my portion in the land of the living." Listen to my cry, for I am in desperate need; rescue me from those who pursue me, for they are too strong for me. Set me free from my prison, that I may praise Your name. Then the righteous will gather about me because of Your goodness to me." —Psalm 142:1-3, 5-7

*Lord, help us learn to pour out our hearts to You, before we are crushed by the weight of our burdens. Help us unload our troubles onto You, before we erupt all over the ones we love. Thank You, Abba Father, for being our Refuge, our Strength, and our Rescue. We love you! Thank You for loving us! In Jesus' name. Amen.* ♡

## *A Heart to Hear*

**JUNE 25 - JULY 1**

## Favorite Fluffy Towel

It's officially summer now. I know this because of the constant pile of wet towels in the laundry room and the corresponding bare shelf in the linen closet.

This morning, I ended up grabbing an old orange towel I took from my grandmother's house when my dad and I packed it up after she passed away. Amazingly, it is still soft and fluffy.

As I picked it up, I was suddenly swept with a longing to be the little girl who used this towel to dry off after swimming in Aunt Ann's pool, the little girl living it up at Grandma's house with no worries except when she will get to swim again.

I thought about it for a moment, and I realized that going back to that time wouldn't really help. Knowing all the things I would have to face all over again made that wish lose its appeal! It hit me that what I really wanted was to know that I am taken care of by someone who loves me unendingly.

My spirit's true longing is for Heaven and my Abba God. His love is the only one that never ends. He will never leave me. He will take care of all the things that worry me. He tells my heart to rest and trust Him; everything is going to be okay. Knowing this, I'm comforted. My heart is warmed, as that little girl wrapped in a cozy orange towel by a loving grandmother.

## A Heart to Hear

Maybe you don't have an orange towel, and maybe you didn't have a grandma like that, but we all have a Father in Heaven who loves us without measure and without end. He has promised to never leave us, and He has put the spirit of adoption in our hearts that enables us to call Him "Daddy God." That is what "Abba" means.

When it was time to close up my grandmother's house, my heart ached. It had been the one constant place in my life. Through the pain, God taught me that home is really just our name for the longing we have to be with Him. We take it with us in our hearts, and one day, we will experience it with all that we are.

So next time you wrap yourself in your favorite fluffy towel, remember you are loved by your Abba Father. He is your home, now and forever! ♡

"For all who are led by the Spirit of God are children of God. So you have not received a spirit that makes you fearful slaves. Instead, you received God's Spirit when he adopted you as his own children. Now we call him, "Abba, Father." For his Spirit joins with our spirit to affirm that we are God's children." —Romans 8:14-16 (NLT)

"Whom have I in heaven but you? And earth has nothing I desire besides you. My flesh and my heart may fail, but God is the strength of my heart and my portion forever." —Psalm 73:25-26 (NIV)

## *A Heart to Hear*

### JULY 2 - 8
## You Never Stand Alone

Relationship status. It's a very significant thing. If you have a Facebook page, you know that your relationship status is one of the first things you fill out on your profile, right alongside your birthday, hometown, political views, and so on. I was reflecting on these words recently and the implications for those whose answer is "single." I know all too well that I am no authority on the subject, but I believe I heard the Lord speak a word of encouragement to those who are.

Single does not mean alone. You are in a relationship with the Lord Jesus, Abba Father, and the Holy Spirit. You never stand alone. You are covered, protected, loved, and cared for.

In my mind's eye, I saw the Lord standing beside a woman with His arm around her shoulders. No matter what our relationship status, any of us can be that woman who feels she is standing alone at times.

These Scriptures speak to the truth of God's faithfulness to be there for us, no matter what.

> When friends can't be found. 2 Timothy 4:16-17
> When parents are no longer there. Psalm 27:10
> When old age comes. Isaiah 46:4
> When rejection happens. Isaiah 54: 4-8

## A Heart to Hear

Our Abba Father loves us, and He wants all of us to know that our relationship with Him is the greatest gift we will ever have. People change, circumstances change, but He never changes. He is Faithful and True, forever and ever.

Amen! Thank You, Lord! ♡

## *A Heart to Hear*

**JULY 9 - 15**

## Be Faithful

*Be faithful.* That is what I hear the Lord saying today. *Be faithful.* He is so faithful to us, and He wants His bride to be faithful to Him.

What does being faithful look like? First, it means that our commitment to Him doesn't waver. We aren't just hanging out until a better offer comes along. We are His, now and forever, no matter what happens.

Our pastor preached last Sunday on storms, those things that unexpectedly show up in our lives and threaten to blow us off course. When a storm comes along we have a choice—faith or fear. Are we going to keep trusting in the One we know to be true, or will our faith crumble in the wind?

Our Heavenly Father is so amazing. Not only can He bring us through the storm, if we will let Him, He can even teach us to dance with Him in the rain.

A dear friend of mine recently allowed me to stand in faith with her as she weathered a severe storm. I watched her do this very thing. She said no to fear and yes to faith, and she put on her dancing shoes. When the Lord utterly defeated the storm, the joy was so sweet because she had never stopped praising Him, even in the darkest hours. That is what being faithful looks like. Faithfulness like this has to be a gift from

## *A Heart to Hear*

God. We don't have it in ourselves, but God has put His Spirit into us and faithfulness is a fruit of His Spirit (Gal. 5:22).

Being faithful also means holding firmly to the truth. The enemy accuses us to the Lord, but he also accuses the Lord to us, constantly trying to get us to doubt God's love and His goodness. We have to hold firmly to the truth—our Abba Father loves us, no matter what happens. This is hard because we all have to fight the fear of what horrible thing He might allow to happen. It is so tempting to live with one eye on the horizon, always watching for that next black cloud. The enemy loves to see us cringing in anticipation of the next blow. That is not the posture of faithfulness!

I've wrestled with this one many times, and I've finally reached the place where I am determined to live in joy, not fear. Painful times will come, but I will not allow the enemy to poison every sunny day with the fear of the hurricane. I'm trusting my Abba Father, my Redeemer, the One who is called Faithful and True. By His grace, I am walking in the sunshine of His love and trusting Him to keep me faithful to the end.

One more thing: *Storm* isn't just a noun; it is also a verb. Instead of hunkering down telling ourselves, "This, too, shall pass," let's go storm the enemy's castle and find some captives who need to be set free! ♡

## *A Heart to Hear*

**JULY 16 - 22**
# Stop Striving

What I hear the Lord saying this week is very succinct and very simple.

*Embrace your helplessness.*

*I will do what I have promised.*

*Stop striving to make it happen.*

*Trust My goodness.*

*Believe I love you.*

*Enjoy the ride.*

Psalm 23. I know you know it, but read it again anyway.

Be blessed, dear sisters, as you soak in His truth. ♡

In His love,
Jennifer

## *A Heart to Hear*

Take the time to jot down all of the ways you have been striving, and then give them all to the Lord.

## *A Heart to Hear*

### JULY 23 - 29
# Strength Big Enough for Every Challenge

As most of you know, my two oldest children have been gone on a mission trip since early July. The last two weeks have felt like such a long time!

Last night, as I was going to sleep, I was praying for my son, David. As I prayed, the Holy Spirit began to shift the theme of my prayer from one of "please smooth his path and make things go well" to "please give him strength big enough for every challenge."

Then, this morning, I was reading in Ephesians, and I found these wonderful verses in chapter three. After looking them up in several different translations, I've decided to share them with you from the *New Living Translation*.

> "I pray that from His glorious, unlimited resources He will empower you with inner strength through His Spirit. Then Christ will make His home in your hearts as you trust in Him. Your roots will grow down into God's love and keep you strong. And may you have the power to understand, as all God's people should, how wide, how long, how high, and how deep His love is. May you experience the love of Christ, though it is too great to understand fully. Then you will be made complete with

## A Heart to Hear

all the fullness of life and power that comes from God."
—Ephesians 3:16-19 (NLT)

God's purpose for us isn't to remove every difficulty from our paths, but to empower us to face every challenge in His mighty strength.

When my children were little and learning to walk, I tried really hard to make sure their paths were free of obstacles and sharp edges. As they have grown up and gone out into the world, I've grudgingly accepted that their paths are full of pitfalls and rough edges that I cannot smooth out for them. They have to learn for themselves how to navigate unfamiliar and sometimes rugged territory. The saving grace is knowing that my Abba Father, the Almighty God, is their Daddy, too, and He is at work in their lives, strengthening each one through His Spirit. He wants to fill them up with the knowledge of His great love and firmly establish their roots in Him.

That is God's purpose in all of us—that we would know Him and that we would be overcomers in Him.

*Yes, Lord, make it so. Let each challenge be just one more incentive to stay close to you, relying on Your power at work in us. In Jesus' name. Amen.* ♡

## *A Heart to Hear*

### JULY 30 - AUGUST 5
### Deny Yourself

*Deny yourself.* Those are not exactly words that bring smiles and warm fuzzies, are they? Trust me, I'd much rather be writing about something else, anything else!

Self-denial is a lost art in our culture. In fact, when I looked up "deny" in the *Webster's 1828 Dictionary,* I found the word "selfdenying" that was dropped from the dictionary in the 1913 update. Isn't that interesting? Almost one hundred years later, the thought of saying no to ourselves is practically unheard of, but that is exactly what Jesus expects us to do. In Luke 9:23 Jesus tells us, "If anyone would come after Me, he must deny himself and take up his cross daily and follow Me."

How does this apply to having a heart to hear? Well, part of learning to hear the Lord is learning to listen even when you don't really like what you hear Him saying. Sometimes He calls us to spend time with Him when we really aren't ready to leave our nice warm beds. He may ask us to give when we'd rather hold on to what is in our hands. Other times, He confronts us with our need to forgive or to ask forgiveness in order to restore a broken relationship. Sometimes He may ask us to give up an indulgence, for a time, as a way of opening our hearts wider to Him.

The Word also makes it clear that Jesus expected that His

## A Heart to Hear

disciples would spend time in prayer and fasting. How often do we listen for the Lord's direction in that area? Ouch, right?

Please understand, I am not advocating tying ourselves up in knots wondering if we are pleasing the Lord every single second of the day. We simply need to live our days with hearts open to the Holy Spirit directing and correcting us.

As I read the Bible, I see that we aren't here simply to enjoy God's blessings and please ourselves. Ephesians 5:15-17 says, "Therefore be careful how you walk, not as unwise men but as wise, making the most of your time, because the days are evil. So then do not be foolish, but understand what the will of the Lord is." Back in Ephesians 2:10, Paul tells us, "We are God's workmanship, created in Christ Jesus to do good works, which God prepared in advance for us to do."

So God has a will for our lives, and He has good works for us to do. Sometimes our hearts will leap to do what He has planned. Other times, we may be begging God for a Plan B! Those are the times when all the practice of denying ourselves pays off. With God's grace, we are able to obey and wait for God's plan to unfold.

*Lord, please give us grace to understand Your will and follow it, especially when it means saying no to our plans and yes to Yours. In Jesus' name. Amen.* ♡

## *A Heart to Hear*

**AUGUST 6 - 12**

## Flourish and Bear Fruit

This morning the Lord is speaking to me in songs. My first born leaves for college tomorrow after returning from a month-long mission trip three days ago! Oy! To say that there is a lot to do is an understatement!

When I looked in the bathroom mirror this morning, I heard these words, "Turn your eyes upon Jesus." I knew the Lord was saying I didn't need to look at my face; I needed to look at His. Those words are from the chorus of an old hymn. Here is the rest of the refrain:

> Turn your eyes upon Jesus,
> Look full in His wonderful face,
> And the things of earth will grow strangely dim,
> In the light of His glory and grace.

I've had my eyes on me and my circumstances: what I need to do—overwhelming; what I can't do—frustrating! I am a drooping branch, down in the dirt trying to be my own vine. I need to be lifted up out of the mud of this earthly struggle, washed clean, and secured once more to the vine where life flows into my little branch. Only then will I flourish and bear fruit, which brings me to the next song.

## *A Heart to Hear*

As I wrote this, I had the faint memory of a song about this very thing from the Newsboys. My sweet husband helped me find it, so here it is. The song is called *Thrive*.

> Will you lift me up with tender care?
> Will you wash me clean in the palm of Your hands?
> Lord, hold me close so I can thrive
> When you touch me, that's when I know I'm alive.

I don't know what each of you is facing today, dear sisters, but I know that it is our Father's heart that we do it in Him.

*Abba Father, we need Your touch, Your presence, Your life flowing through us. You are the Master Gardener. Please touch us and enable us to thrive. In Jesus' name. Amen.* ♡

## *A Heart to Hear*

AUGUST 13 - 19
# Kudzu

Last Wednesday, my daughter, Catherine, and I hit the road to drive from Texas to South Carolina to take her to college. It was definitely bittersweet, but I was so grateful for the time together as we drove one thousand miles.

We moved her in on Friday and made one more Walmart run and delivery on Saturday. I got my last hug from her until Christmas, and come Sunday morning, I was worshipping with my parents at their church in Virginia.

In the presence of the Lord, my tightly checked emotions came undone. However, despite feeling incredibly homesick for my girl, I was so aware of God's overwhelming goodness. As I reflected on how blessed I have been in so many ways, I heard the Lord saying, *I came to give you life and life more abundantly.* Jesus said those words in John 10:10.

"Abundantly." This is an awesome word. It means "excessive in quantity, superior in quality, profuse, overflowing, more than enough." You could even say "extravagant." Abundance is something God has built in to His creation.

If you've driven down the highway through Tennessee and Arkansas, like I just did, you've seen an abundance of Kudzu. That's the name for that out-of-control vine that engulfs telephone poles, trees, and sometimes entire hillsides. That is

## *A Heart to Hear*

what abundant looks like! God's desire is to give us life that is abundant, not a little houseplant we struggle to keep alive. He wants His life in us to engulf everything and everyone around us with His goodness.

He is the only one who makes life worth living. I am so glad He tore in two the veil that separated us from Him! I am so thankful that He sent Jesus to be Emmanuel, God with us, the Way Maker, the Redeemer! Alleluia! He redeems all the hard things, the bad things, all the evil things that touch us. He is the one who heals, restores, and renews. He brings abundant life! He is our hope.

He forgives and gives us grace to do the same. He makes life worth living, and death something to look forward to because it just means even more of Him.

Dear ones, embrace the abundance of Abba Father's love for you. Revel in it. Float on it. Dive down deep into it. Rest in it. He loves you, and He has life for you.

*Abba, You are so good. Jesus, You are so good. Holy Spirit, You are so good. Open our hearts to believe and receive all the life You want to pour into us. Enable us to share it with everyone we meet. In Jesus' name. Amen.* ♡

## *A Heart to Hear*

AUGUST 20 - 26
# Fresh Start

Monday was the first day of the new school year for my children. Now, I know not everyone who reads this has school age children, but surely we all remember the anticipation and apprehension that filled our hearts on the first day each year.

I saw a comment on Facebook the other day from a friend who found herself drawn to the school supply aisle despite the fact that no one in her house needed them. Who can resist the allure of a new box of crayons, fresh notebooks, and pens? Anything is possible! It is a new year and a fresh opportunity to be the person inside that no one has yet seen.

I believe our Abba Father knew we would need fresh starts in our lives. I love that His Word promises us His mercies are new every morning. Just the fact that we get to go to bed, put yesterday behind us, and awake to a new day is a mercy in itself.

The change of the seasons is another refreshing touch a loving God built into our lives. My energy and hope are always renewed in the fall when the weather starts to cool. While we are still waiting for that blessed change here in Texas, I am encouraged to know that God's grace for today is freshly baked and ready for consumption! The Word tells us that Jesus is the Bread of Life. He is the Source of the grace by which we stand. It isn't our merit, our ability, or our performance.

## *A Heart to Hear*

We stand on the solid Rock of the righteousness Jesus lived out on our behalf.

So … if you need a fresh start today, throw yourself once again on the mercy of our loving Father and receive the grace that cleanses us from all our unrighteousness and empowers us to step forth in hope and trust that today really will be different. Then, go get that box of new crayons, and color something that makes you smile!

Study: Lamentations 3:22-24; Romans 5:1-2; John 6:32-35

*Abba, thank You for Your faithful love. Draw us to yourself. Renew our hearts. Restore our souls. For Your Name's sake. Amen.* ♡

## A Heart to Hear

**AUGUST 27 - SEPTEMBER 2**

# Let It Go!

"Let it go, let it roll right off your shoulder. Don't you know the hardest part is over?" Those are the first lines of a song called "Little Wonders." This song plays at the end of the Disney film "Meet the Robinsons." I love the song, and I love the movie because it illustrates so clearly the negative effect holding on to the hurts of the past can have on our lives. The movie tells the story of two orphaned boys and how their lives unfold as one learns to keep moving forward, while the other spends his entire life looking back on one moment of disappointment.

Isaiah 43:18-19 tell us, "Forget the former things; do not dwell on the past. See, I am doing a new thing! Now it springs up; do you not perceive it? I am making a way in the desert and streams in the wasteland."

Forgetting the things of the past is an accomplishment that can only come from God. To get to this place, we have to admit we have been wounded and patiently let the wound heal. If there is still a thorn, we have to be willing to let our Abba Father pull it out, even though it hurts.

We also have to let go of our right to prosecute the offender. We have to turn them over to the One who had mercy on us and trust His justice and mercy on them. Only

## *A Heart to Hear*

then are we free to begin to forget, to let it go, to quit prodding the sore spot, to move forward in freedom.

I'd like to close by sharing some thoughts the Lord spoke on this subject to my husband recently during worship:

> There is a gift of forgetfulness—the ability to not remember, to let it go, to lose the encumbrance of burdens and heaviness of pains and failures so that they no longer affect you. Those pains, scars, and memories affect how you live your life. To forget these things removes their influence.

What a promise. What an opportunity. What a gift!

*Lord God, help us forget the former things and embrace the new things You are doing. Thank You for being a God who makes roads in the desert and streams in the wilderness. We love You! Amen.* ♡

# *A Heart to Hear*

### SEPTEMBER 3 - 9
## Crock Pot or Microwave?

Okay, I have a confession to make: I really love watching competitive cooking shows on television. I know they manufacture drama, and I really wish the contestants had a wider vocabulary, but for someone whose culinary adventures consist mainly of finding yet another way to cook chicken, it is a window to another world.

I never plan to prepare squab or pork belly, but I am fascinated by those who do and actually make it look delicious. One of the most consistent challenges for the chefs is to create something amazing in an extremely short amount of time. I really enjoy watching those poor folks run around the kitchen, chopping and cooking like mad, trying to bring their dishes to completion before the timer goes off. It's nice to see somebody else struggling to put a meal on the table, while I sit and watch for a change!

What does any of this have to do with hearing God? Well, lately, I've been wondering if I am experiencing the refiner's fire, or if I am simply simmering away in a stew of my own making. Maybe it's a little bit of both. Of one thing I am certain: God's ways tend to be more crock pot than microwave.

I desire complete transformation in minutes. My Abba Father seems comfortable with letting things sit on the back

## A Heart to Hear

burner, bubbling up now and then, for years on end. Why does it take so long for some issues to get dealt with? Why doesn't He just zap those folks that are driving me crazy—especially that woman in the mirror?

My dad likes to say that the secret ingredient for making something delicious is time. The longer you wait for it, the sweeter the pie. I think the Lord must have the same idea. Over and over, the Bible encourages us to wait patiently for the Lord. Psalm 27:14 tells us, "Wait for the LORD; be strong and take heart and wait for the LORD." Isaiah 40:31 (KJV) says, "They that wait upon the LORD shall renew their strength; they shall mount up with wings as eagles; they shall run, and not be weary; and they shall walk, and not faint."

What I hear the Lord saying to us is simply this: *Wait on Me. Trust Me even when you don't understand what I'm doing and you wonder why it takes so long. When My work is complete, it will be worth the wait!* ♡

"For our light, momentary affliction (this slight distress of the passing hour) is ever more and more abundantly preparing and producing and achieving for us an everlasting weight of glory [beyond all measure, excessively surpassing all comparisons and all calculations, a vast and transcendent glory and blessedness never to cease!]" —2 Corinthians 4:17 (AMP)

# *A Heart to Hear*

SEPTEMBER 10 - 16

## Get A Grip!

A couple of things happened to me today that really got me thinking about the importance of holding on tightly to what is important. First, my daughter's alarm clock went off an hour early. She turned it off and went back to sleep. I, on the other hand, was effectively awakened and immediately wondered if the Lord hadn't given me a good opportunity to spend some time getting up to date with Him. The mental debate was over when I remembered a verse that says "a little sleep, a little slumber ... so shall poverty come upon you like an armed man" (Prov. 6:9-11).

When I got to my quiet time chair, my heart was heavy over the lack of training I've given my own children in the Word of God. I know that verse because my dad made me study Psalms and Proverbs continually. *(Thanks, Dad. Sorry I was so grouchy at morning Bible time.)*

My second wake-up call came from a series of articles I read about parenting by a man who really spoke the truth. He talked about the need for mothers to know the difference between being nurturing versus being solely Nurturers with a capital "N." He spoke of the need to get comfortable with being in authority over my children and not hesitating to say "because I said so." It was like a breath of fresh air and a strong cup of

## A Heart to Hear

coffee. I felt refreshed, encouraged, and ready to get a grip.

As I sat down to write today, that phrase kept rolling around in my mind. I feel the need to get a grip on the truth and get it into my heart, my head, and especially my backbone. I struggle with being easily swayed by others and easily distracted by anything and everything. My convictions are constantly being tested and my decisions are often disputed, especially by my teenagers! My thoughts accuse me, and so does the devil. I desperately need the truth of God's Word to keep me straight and standing firm. I need to keep a tight hold on it because it's incredibly valuable. Knowing the truth is the source of my freedom (Jn. 8:32). Keeping my mind fixed on the Lord is the source of my peace (Is. 26:3). Viewing my circumstances from an eternal perspective is the source of my hope (Ro. 8:18). Remembering I have been chosen and I'm unconditionally loved by Almighty God is the source of my joy (Eph. 1:3-14).

These are my treasures, and they are far more valuable than any amount of money. They can't be stolen from me, but if I don't remember I have them, I'm like the lady who not only forgot where she hid her mad money, she forgot she had it in the first place! (Not that this has ever happened to me!)

Let's get a grip—on the Word of God and His truth. It is more valuable than a pocket full of diamonds or a diversified investment portfolio! Remember, He never loosens His grip on us. In fact, Jesus promises us in John 10:28 that no one can ever snatch us out of His hand.

There's just one more thing. When I asked the Lord what He wanted to say to you today, He told me to tell you *He loves you very much!* ♡

## *A Heart to Hear*

**SEPTEMBER 17 - 23**
# Walking the Tightrope

When I sit down at my computer, I usually do three things: check my email, take a look at Facebook, and glance at the headlines on Foxnews.com. If I'm feeling frivolous, I also look at Yahoo. This gives me what's going on with me, my friends, the world, and that odd third wheel in all our lives—the media/entertainment industry.

By the time I'm done with the news headlines, I'm often so discouraged by all the tragedies, disasters, and frightening reports of rising tyrants and coming plagues I can barely get up and start a load of laundry. It's difficult to reconcile myself to a world where I want to be happy over the little joys in life, like getting a really good parking spot at Walmart, while in the back of my mind, I'm wondering how long before the fragile house of cards of our world's economic and political balance comes tumbling down.

The question that keeps rolling around in my head is this: "How do I live in this world? How do I walk this tightrope between time and eternity?"

When I expressed some of these thoughts to my husband, he directed me to Psalm 73. Our pastor preached from this passage recently in a sermon on handling stress spiritually—a very timely word.

## *A Heart to Hear*

As the psalmist states, trying to understand this world is a wearisome task until I enter into the sanctuary of God. When I shut out the world and enter into the presence of the Lord, I begin to see everything more clearly (Ps.73:17). I don't know what is coming my way tomorrow, next year, or even today, but I do know Who is holding my hand (Ps. 73:23). He is faithful. He is my refuge, my safe place. I may be on a tightrope, but the Lord Almighty is my Father, and He is holding my hand. Romans 8 tells me that He will cause every circumstance I face to work for good in my life because I am His. It also assures me that nothing can ever separate me from my Father's love.

Bottom line, I think the answer to my question is stated pretty clearly in the wise words of the retiring preacher to the newly hired fellow, "Plant a tree, but keep your suitcase under the bed." My dad repeated those words often as a reminder that we are to fully invest ourselves in where we are, but always keep in mind that the assignment may not be permanent.

Let's live as oaks of righteousness, repairers of the ruined places (Is. 61:1-4), but always remembering this earth is not our final destination.

*Abba, please help us stay aware of Your loving hand holding us up, no matter what. Give us hearts that treasure Your Word and draw life from it daily. In Jesus' name. Amen.* ♡

# *A Heart to Hear*

**SEPTEMBER 24 - 30**
# Poison Darts

Poison darts, pierced hearts, and birthday candles. These are the things on my mind today. I've just been reading Sharon Hinck's *Restorer* series. I have a weakness for fiction, as anyone close to me could tell you. Books are a controlled substance at my house because I am a recovering read-a-holic. Seriously, my children say "kid on fire" to get my attention when I have a book in my hand!

Anyway, these books have really blessed me because of the way the author is able to weave biblical truth into her story. I came away from reading the first book, *The Restorer*, with a much greater awareness of the need to keep the Word of God in my mind, my heart, and on my tongue. In the story, the only way to counteract the mind poison of the enemy is by speaking the Verses given by The One.

For us, it is no different. The enemy is always shooting his poison darts at our hearts, causing pain, confusion, and sometimes taking us out of the battle completely for a while. That happened to me last week. I wrote the truth, but I didn't do a very good job of walking in it. The enemy sent his stinging arrows into an area of past wounding, and I was a mess for the rest of the week. I hate to admit it, but there it is.

## A Heart to Hear

As my husband is fond of pointing out, the devil is a jerk, and he doesn't fight fair. He doesn't wait for us to pick up our swords before he begins his assault. He attacks the weak, the young, the hurting, and the defenseless. That is why none of us get too far in life without some scars on our hearts.

Praise God, our Redeemer is a Healer of wounded hearts. That is just one more reason to love Him. He is the One who came to set captives free and heal broken hearts.

If you need to be reminded why our God is the only One worthy of adoration, read Isaiah 61. He is the One we need. He is a God to fear, but not to be afraid of. You can trust Him with all that you have and all that you are. He made you, like Build-A-Bear, but better! He designed you. He put every little unique detail in place. You are custom, one-of-a-kind, His creation, and He's proud of you. Just as tenderly as a mother treasures every stumbling step her baby takes, He loves every single step our hearts take in faith toward Him, even those we take on trembling legs.

Today is my birthday, and Abba Father gave me a wonderful gift. He gave me the truth I just shared with you: *He made me, He loves me, and it's okay to be me. He likes me like I am!*

Sometimes, okay many times, I have wished I were more like someone else. I wish for a different personality, a different appearance, even a different sense of style. I long to be carefree instead of careful, quicker to laugh instead of cry, a daring adventurer instead of a die-hard bookworm, but my Abba Father told me it's okay to be who He made me.

This is the truth my wounded heart needed to hear. He

## *A Heart to Hear*

loves me. That makes blowing out all those birthday candles a true celebration. Besides, who knows what I will be like by the time He gets through with me? In the meantime, I plan to enjoy the ride, and I'm going to try to remember to keep my shield up and my sword close by! ♡

"Instead of their shame my people will receive a double portion, and instead of disgrace they will rejoice in their inheritance; and so they will inherit a double portion in their land, and everlasting joy will be theirs." —Isaiah 61:7

"I delight greatly in the LORD; my soul rejoices in my God. For He has clothed me with garments of salvation and arrayed me in a robe of righteousness ..." —Isaiah 61:10a

## *A Heart to Hear*

List some of the poison darts the enemy sends your way and the truth that counteracts them:

## *A Heart to Hear*

OCTOBER 1 - 7
# Feeling Weary?

Anybody besides me feeling weary? The calendar pages are relentlessly turning. Soon the holiday season will be upon us.

Life is ramping up to its most hectic pace. Political debates are heating up as important elections draw near. Students are neck deep in their studies. The schedule is packed with sporting events, competitions, fundraising festivals, and more. Illness, grief, challenging relationships, family members, and our own moody selves are all demanding our attention. Additionally, we face a constant barrage of everything from discouraging thoughts to outright physical attacks from the enemy of our souls. No wonder I need a second cup of coffee!

As I turned my heart to the Lord this morning and opened up the Psalms, I was comforted to see the psalmist expressing his heart with a sigh. It's nice to know I'm not the only one. Many times David uttered the words, "How long, O Lord, how long?"

If this is the cry of your heart today, you are not alone. I believe our Abba Father wants us to be comforted by the fact that He knows how we feel. He is listening. He is patient, even when we constantly ask Him, "Are we there yet?"

The word He is giving me today is *perseverance*. To persevere is to keep doing what you've set out to do, to be

## A Heart to Hear

steadfast, constant. Those aren't words we hear very often in our society anymore, but they represent a virtue we need now more than ever. Look at the words of the Apostle Peter in 1 Peter 5:8-10:

> "Be self-controlled and alert. Your enemy the devil prowls around like a roaring lion looking for someone to devour. Resist him, standing firm in the faith, because you know that your brothers throughout the world are undergoing the same kind of sufferings. And the God of all grace, who called you to his eternal glory in Christ, after you have suffered a little while, will himself restore you and make you strong, firm and steadfast."

It isn't in ourselves that we become steadfast. It is only in abiding in our Lord, keeping our minds fixed on Him. As Isaiah 26:3 promises, "You will keep in perfect peace him whose mind is steadfast, because he trusts in you." This steadfast trust requires an active mind, not a passive one. You could compare it to maintaining proper posture. Slouching mentally can so quickly lead to slumping emotionally. Let's purpose to live uprightly in mind and spirit. Life is often exhausting, but it is also beautiful. Part of that beauty is the loveliness of constancy which is revealed as we faithfully fill our places simply for the glory of God.

*Lord, please renew our strength as we wait on you. Enable us to be faithful to the end. Encourage our hearts to trust You even in the hard things we don't understand. In the name of Jesus, our Redeemer. Amen.* ♡

## *A Heart to Hear*

OCTOBER 8-14
## Laser-Guided Missile

Last year, before I began writing a weekly word, the ladies at my church received a word of encouragement that came from Sarah Young's excellent book, *Jesus Calling*, published by Thomas Nelson. I haven't read it much since I began writing simply because I didn't want to end up writing like Sarah instead of myself. However, during the past couple of days, I have been in a battle. I picked up *Jesus Calling* because I needed to hear something that would speak straight to my heart. I definitely found what I needed. What I read was like a precision missile targeted straight for my heart. (Have I mentioned how much my husband loves the Military Channel?) Anyway, it was a direct hit, and I feel that the truth I found there is what we need to hear today. I encourage you to get a copy of Sarah's book and read the entry for October 10. Actually, you should read it all because it is wonderful! Due to copyright restrictions, I can't give you Sarah's words here, but this is what I took away from what she had to say.

We need to remember that whether we feel like it or not, the amazing, light-filled Presence of the Lord is always surrounding us. His love never leaves us. When we take our eyes off Him and Who He is in our present circumstances and begin to try to figure out how we are going to get through the

## A Heart to Hear

day, the month, or even the year ahead, we are really saying we think we can get along without Him. Planning, predicting, and even trying to control what will happen comes naturally to most humans. We have to remember, however, that there is only One whose name is All-Sufficient, and it's not us!

Our Abba Father wants our trust. He tells us to enter His rest. He wants us to bring Him our worries, our needs, even our fears, and lay them down at His feet. Some days, I find myself needing to do this over and over. I pour out my need, and I receive His peace, His love, and the grace to believe that He will supply whatever I need for that moment. This is what living in relationship with the Lord is all about. Psalm 37:3-5, 7 tells puts it beautifully:

> "Trust in the Lord, and do good; dwell in the land and cultivate faithfulness. Delight yourself in the Lord; and He will give you the desires of your heart. Commit your way to the Lord. Trust also in Him and He will do it. Rest in the Lord and wait patiently for Him."

Trust the Lord. Trust His timing. Trust His provision. Trust Him to be bigger than your own mistakes or those of others. He is the One Who alone does all things well. He will complete His work in us.

*Abba Father, help us to trust You. Help our unbelief. Heal our wounds and scars. Bring glory and honor to Your name in every aspect of our lives. Through Jesus, our Redeemer. Amen.* ♡

## *A Heart to Hear*

**OCTOBER 15 - 21**
## Overcomers In Training

Late last week, I was musing on the hard things of life and thinking about how I pray. Too many times my response to hard things is to pray for immediate, miraculous relief. I'm not one of those people who says, "I have a headache. Maybe God has something to teach me through suffering." Usually, I take some Advil and pray for the pain to stop. Unless the Lord directs me otherwise I don't think there's anything wrong with that, but lately God is opening my eyes to praying from a different mental base camp than the one of "Painless as Possible, Please!"

This new mental base camp is called "Overcomers in Training." Over there, they embrace the idea that earth is the training ground where the righteous learn to rule and reign with Christ. They understand it is a marathon obstacle course, not a series of spa retreats. They are about becoming conquerors, not being air-lifted by angels over every rock in the path. They are tough-minded, as opposed to hardheaded.

Yes, it is foreign territory I haven't really wanted to explore! However, I can no longer ignore all the evidence in Scripture that indicates this is where our Abba Father really expects the body of Christ to live. James 1:12 tells us, "Blessed is the man who perseveres under trial, because when he has stood the test, he will receive the crown of life that God has promised to those

## *A Heart to Hear*

who love Him." The book of Revelation is filled with wonderful promises to those who overcome. Check some of them out in chapters 2 and 3. To overcome means "to win despite obstacles." That is what we are called to do.

How does this change the way I pray? For starters, it takes my focus away from looking for the exit in times of trial and onto looking for the opportunity my Heavenly Father is giving me. The only way to build muscle is by lifting increasingly heavier weights. The only way for my faith to grow is through the continual process of facing trials, where the only answer is to trust the Lord and His strength to bring me through, especially when it doesn't make any sense. Some people say, "If God would explain this to me, then I would trust Him," but a trust that requires explanations isn't trust at all. It's scary to commit those words to print. Even now, the enemy is whispering in my ear, "Will you still say that when your Abba Father allows you to experience something really devastating?" To that, I can only say my prayer is that God will enable me to be faithful to Him until the end. I pray that He will help me recognize and reject the lies of the enemy. I pray that He will give me His strength to do the hard things, and the wisdom to know that everything is hard when I am not walking in Him. In the meantime, I'm looking to get comfortable with not being comfortable and learning to endure hardship as the discipline that comes to all sons and soldiers. Hoorah!

*Father God, please help us grow strong roots that go down deep into You. Give us brave hearts that trust You even through hard times. In Jesus' mighty name. Amen.* ♡

## *A Heart to Hear*

OCTOBER 22 - 28
## Wormy Apples

I've been praying and listening for a word for us this week. Sometimes it flows so easily, but this is not one of those times! This morning only one phrase kept running through my head, and it wasn't Scripture! All I could hear, over and over, was "Devil with a blue dress on ..." Some of you might be familiar with that old song. Some of you might be saying, "What???" Anyway, as I've pondered this, I believe I'm supposed to share today about how the devil rarely shows up looking like the evil one that he is. Like the wicked queen offering Snow White a lovely apple, the devil hardly ever tries to get us to swallow something labeled "Poison." No, he is the original marketer, and his plans for our destruction are usually hidden in an inviting package.

Self-pity doesn't march up waving a flag that says, "Feel sorry for yourself! You can be more miserable than you already are!" No, it slinks up beside us, full of sweet sympathy, "Oh, poor you, no one understands, do they? No one cares how hard you work, and no one notices your needs. How sad ..."

Before we know it, anger and blame have joined the party, too. Unforgiveness comes disguised as a black leather jacket called "being strong." It looks good, and it makes you feel tough, but in reality it takes more strength to release someone

## *A Heart to Hear*

than it does to hold on to bitterness. Many people stomp around in their own strength and self-reliance, never realizing the heaviness they feel is because of their own choice not to let go of the hurts of the past.

One more rotten apple in the devil's basket is exclusivity. Like a lovely, ivy-covered brick wall, this is the one that says, "Isn't our little circle of friends perfect? We don't really need to take a chance on including someone new, do we?" The devil is so happy to keep us behind our walls wrapped in our comfy blankets of complacency. He doesn't want us thinking about how it feels to be new or to need a friend.

Those are just a few of the wormy apples the devil would love for us to bite into. They look like treats, but they are really the dirtiest of tricks. Speaking of tricks and treats, I just need to say it: I hate Halloween! I am so ready for November to arrive and to see all the stupid ghosts, goblins, and giant spiders go away. I hate it because, in my mind, it relegates evil to something fun and imaginary. I've seen and experienced too much devastation at the hands of the enemy to ever consider evil cute. Dear sisters, stay alert. Watch out for the tricks and schemes of the evil one. Don't give yourself a pass to harbor an attitude you know is ungodly. Be ruthless in your rejection of evil, and be relentless in your pursuit of the One Who alone gives life.

*Abba Father, please give us eyes to see past the devil's disguises. Give us wisdom to sidestep his snares. Keep us on the narrow path, even when the wide one is so alluring. In Jesus' name. Amen.* ♡

# *A Heart to Hear*

**OCTOBER 29 - NOVEMBER 4**

## Don't Throw Away Your Confidence

I'm writing this the day before a major election day. Tomorrow, we will all know how election day turned out. For now, I'm just glad to know that our Abba Father, our Daddy God, already knows what all our tomorrows hold, and He has promised to be with us to sustain us by His grace through each one.

The word today is simple: *Hold on.* Hold on to your confidence in the Lord and His goodness. Hebrews 10:35 urges us, "So do not throw away your confidence; it will be richly rewarded." Hold on to your hope. Where is our hope? Our hope is in the blood of Jesus as the payment for our sin. Our hope is in the redemption of our failures and the promise God made to complete His work in us. Our hope is in the resurrection of our bodies and the transformation of them into something that will never decay or die. Our hope is in the renewal of all things and the utter defeat of evil. Hope is not a wispy tissue we use to dab our eyes as we wish for something better. Hope is a good strong rope, endlessly useful and absolutely necessary. Hold on to it!

Hold on to the Word of God. Romans 15:4 tells us: "For everything that was written in the past was written to teach us, so that through endurance and the encouragement of the

## A Heart to Hear

Scriptures we might have hope."

We also need to be sure we hold on to what the Lord has already done for us. Every personal word of encouragement, every answered prayer, every time the Lord has come through for us in big ways or small, we should hold on to each one as we would to a precious jewel. These are our treasures, and they are worth far more than diamonds or rubies. The people of Israel were often encouraged to remember what God had done for them. Too many times they ended up forgetting His mighty works on their behalf. How often do we do the same?

Finally, we must hold on to each another. There are times when it feels like we are lost at sea, desperately clinging to our little pieces of wreckage until the rescue boat arrives. Those of us with a little firmer grip must hang on to those whose heads are going under. We need each other. You never know when the next wave is coming in your direction. In Romans 15:5-6 Paul prays for us, "May the God who gives endurance and encouragement give you a spirit of unity among yourselves as you follow Christ Jesus, so that with one heart and mouth you may glorify the God and Father of our Lord Jesus Christ."

*Yes, Lord! Please make us one. Help us remember our enemy is not flesh and blood. Father, help us hold on to You and to each other. Help us cling to what is good and reject the useless things that waste our time. Help us remember all that You have done. Keep us faithful to our journey's end. For your glory. In Jesus' name. Amen.* ♡

# *A Heart to Hear*

**NOVEMBER 5 - 11**

# Ouch!

There are times when this world fools me into believing it is home. Like the old cartoon with the sheepdog guarding the peaceful meadow, all seems right with the world. The sun is shining, puffy clouds float in the sky, a lovely melody plays in the background when, suddenly, a lamb is yanked off its feet by the wolf who has been creeping up all along.

Once again I am slapped in the face with the reality that I live on a battleground in disguise. Around the world, our brothers and sisters in Christ face the adversary on many different fronts. For some it means risking their lives to confess the name of Jesus as their Savior. For others it means open battle with witchcraft and sorcery in places where power and religion go hand in hand.

Here in America, our battle is much harder to discern. We wake up warm and safe. No one is throwing grenades in our neighborhoods or seeking to lock up our churches, at least not openly. Our biggest threats are apathy and self-absorption. We are simply too busy doing our own thing to care much about our place in the Kingdom of God. We are more interested in the Kingdom as a kind of enhancement to our lives rather than the very essence of why we live. We want peace, protection, and blessing to shine down from on high while we go about

## A Heart to Hear

our business without being bothered too much.

Ouch! My toes are feeling pretty trampled right about now, and this little weekly word is heading in a direction I'm not sure I want to go.

Here is what I think the Lord is saying to us today: *Your prayer is "Thy Kingdom come, Thy will be done," but are your hearts really desiring My will and My Kingdom?*

Are our lives really focused on bringing the Kingdom—His rule and reign—to where we live? Am I asking Abba Father, Who is also Adonai—Master, Owner, Lord—to come and set up His rule right here in the middle of my living room? Honestly, I don't think I know what "living for His Kingdom" looks like, and frankly, I'm a little scared to find out. On the other hand, wouldn't it be ridiculous to squander our lives on the temporary instead of pouring ourselves out for the Eternal and His purposes, which will never fail?

*Abba, Adonai, please turn our hearts again to You. Please stop our spinning and help us focus on You and Your Kingdom. Please show each one of us what that means in our moment by moment lives. Give us hearts that desire Your eternal Kingdom above our own temporary ones. In Jesus' name. Amen.* ♡

## *A Heart to Hear*

**NOVEMBER 12-18**

# Whisper or Megaphone?

Over the weekend, my husband and I were blessed to visit our nation's capital together. He had planned to go early to do some sightseeing before attending business meetings this week, and I was happily able to join him, thanks to help from dear friends to ensure the well-being of our children in our absence. It is not an easy thing to get away as a couple when you have children, especially as many as we have! I had been asking the Lord to give us some special time together for several months, so this truly felt like a gift from Him as all the details rapidly fell into place.

Washington, D.C., is an amazing city filled with wonders. The history of our country literally stares you right in the face. One of the most striking features of the city is all the memorials to those whose blood has been spilled for this land. The solemn sense of sacrifice sits heavily on those places. Gratitude to God and to all who have served to help us become and remain a free nation filled my heart continually.

As I listened to the Lord for us this week, one word settled into my mind: *sensitivity*. I have searched my online dictionaries, and "to be sensitive" means simply "to be responsive to outside stimulus." *Sensitivity* can be defined as "consideration or responsiveness." I think what the Holy Spirit

## *A Heart to Hear*

is saying is simply for us to become more responsive to His still, small voice.

I don't know about you, but I've often longed for God to cast aside the subtlety and write on the sky, to forgo the whisper and grab a megaphone. However, I believe Jesus wants a Bride who is in tune with His Spirit to such a degree that the slightest touch on our hearts gets our attention. The unspoken word, the look that says all, the small tilt of the head, these are the communication tools of deep relationships, of lovers. I think the Lord is looking for this in us, His Bride.

This is not a call to tie yourself in knots trying to hear what you can't. It is simply an invitation to be open to the idea that when God speaks in the quietest of ways, it is because He wants to know we will incline our hearts to Him, eager to hear His words. Of course, this is something only He can do in us, but He wants to, and He will, if we let Him.

*Yes, Lord, we want to be aware of your voice speaking in all ways. Please give us ears to hear Your voice, no matter how still or small. Please help us respond, knowing Your strength will enable us to do what You ask. We will not draw back in fear, but we will come in confidence, knowing You alone are good. In Jesus' name. Amen.* ♡

## *A Heart to Hear*

**NOVEMBER 19 - 25**

# Give Thanks in All Circumstances

Thanks giving—let's do it! I have been enjoying catching up with a "friend of long standing," which is not the same as an "old friend," or so she tells me! I'm feeling the joy of shared laughter with someone who has known me for a long time. It's a blessing, and I'm so grateful!

Thank You, Lord, for giving us the gift of friendship. Building good ones is never easy. Sometimes the road is rocky, and I'm not talking about ice cream, although that can help! Being a good friend is tough. It requires of us that we lower our defenses, risk a bit, and sometimes get hurt. The pain is part of it. We hurt when our friends let us down, which should only be occasionally or else it's probably time to evaluate the health of the relationship. We hurt when they hurt. All in all, this business of caring about other people and letting them into our lives isn't for the faint of heart, but it is so rewarding.

I hope you have friends to be thankful for this year. If not, I pray that our Abba Father gives you the grace to find those you can trust with your true self, and the courage to do it.

Another blessing I am most thankful for is our church family. I read a quote recently from long ago about the satisfaction of living in a village where everyone knows and is interested in you, and you know and are interested in

## A Heart to Hear

everyone. Our church immediately came to my mind. This is our village, a place where we are known and cared for, a refuge from the anonymity of the city, our spiritual hometown. The local church is God's gift to us! We all must do our part to keep the warmth of our village alive. This means praying God's best for one another, not just ourselves, holding out caring hands in hard times, and humbly speaking the truth in love when it is needed. If we all pick up the trash we see, the building will stay clean. If we all stay current with one another by forgiving offenses when they come, extending grace where it is needed, our collective heart stays clean and open to what the Lord desires to do among us.

I'd like to close by encouraging you to read Ephesians 4. The Lord took me there this week, and it is so relevant to where we are, so grab your Bible and read it! Then, if you're like me, you'll probably need to read it again, and again. Blessings on you, dear sisters!

*Thank You, Lord, for the gift our church is to us. Help us to be willing to invest ourselves in the building up in love of this expression of the body of Christ. Thank You for each and every living soul. Please enable us to grow up together in unity, maturity, and the fullness of Christ. Give us your love for one another. Help us bear each other's burdens and bring healing to each one's wounds. Give us courage to truly love You and each other.* ♡

"Rejoice always, pray continually, give thanks in all circumstances; for this is God's will for you in Christ Jesus."
—1 Thessalonians 5:16-18

# *A Heart to Hear*

**NOVEMBER 26 - DECEMBER 2**
## What I Can Give

Here we are, poised on the brink of the Advent season, like a roller coaster at the peak of the first hill. Now more than ever, we need to hear the Lord! Everywhere we turn, voices are shouting for our attention, our time, and our money. Pleas for giving to those in need compete with commercials touting the latest trends in toys. The desire to focus on simply celebrating the birth of Christ collides with a calendar that is suddenly covered with special events. Most stressful of all is trying to figure out what will bring joy to each and every person on our lists without causing a financial meltdown.

Suddenly the joy of the season is wavering as we take up the burden of making Christmas wonderful for all the people we love. Does anybody besides me tremble a little at the daunting task of decorating, planning, shopping, cooking, cleaning, baking, gift wrapping, gift giving, memory making, and don't forget photographing and scrapbooking the whole thing? *Oy vey!*

So ... here in my quiet place, I'm coming to the Lord, and I'm asking Him to make my mind new about Christmas. Ephesians 4:23 tells us to let the Spirit renew our thoughts and attitudes. When it comes to preparing my heart for Christmas, that's exactly what I need Him to do.

## *A Heart to Hear*

First on the agenda is dealing with the fear I feel over wanting to make everyone happy and being pretty sure I will fail. When I brought these fears to the Lord, He told me gently, yet firmly, that He alone is responsible for each living soul. He said, "You can love, care, and do what I allow you to do, but you will NEVER be able to make them happy or holy or whole. This is MY work. You are required to trust Me and stay out of My Way!"

There are many things I can give my family for Christmas, but happiness is not one of them. What I can give them is myself, at peace, simply loving them with no guilt, no stress, and no strings. I can give them freedom to be who God is making them to be. I can give them the gift of enjoying the imperfect instead of driving everyone crazy in my obsession to make everything flawless.

One more deep breath, and I think I'm ready to look forward to Christmas. My heart feels lighter because I know now that my Abba Father has His own plans for this special season, and He alone is able to make Christmas exactly what it needs to be for each one that I love. ♡

"Every good and perfect gift is from above, coming down from the Father of the heavenly lights, who does not change like shifting shadows." — James 1:17

# A Heart to Hear

DECEMBER 3 - 9

## Roll With It

Last week, I wrote about my need to give my Christmas stress to the Lord and trust Him to work His wonders in the lives of everyone I love. My husband told me he was excited about seeing me walk that out. Thankfully, I was able to give that expectation to the Lord, too, and actually trust Him to change me instead of trying to grind it out myself. The really good news is that He's already doing it! My husband told me today that he actually sees a difference in me. Yippee! Over the weekend, I had plenty of opportunities to put this into practice as my agenda got changed, plans had to be laid aside, and a great many things suddenly got added to my to-do list. Somehow (I think it was grace), I was able to roll with it and just do what needed to be done. I was able to trust that all the things that needed to happen would happen, and the things that had to get tossed weren't really essential anyway. This is a major hallelujah moment for me. For so many years, I felt like I was slogging through thick mud up to my knees—everything was hard. Now, life feels more like a dance workout than calisthenics. It's hard, and I'm still sweating, but I'm having fun. Walking in grace makes all the difference!

When the angel came to the shepherds and scared them half to death the night Jesus was born he said, "Fear not, for

## *A Heart to Hear*

behold, I bring you good tidings of great joy." That is what Jesus' birth means for us—an exchange of our fears for His gift of great joy, the joy that comes from being utterly forgiven and completely set free from fear. He came to commute our death sentence, to take the ax that was going to fall on our necks. Not only that, He came to show us our Abba Father.

Many people see God like the old Far Side cartoon: a grumpy old man in the sky just waiting to hit the "smite" button and blow us away. No! Our God is the One who told the angel to say, "Don't be scared. I've got good news for all people." He is the One who says, "I've sent you a Savior, a Redeemer. I don't want anyone to die in their sin. I want to cleanse you, forgive you, and bring you home to live with Me. In fact, I want to put My Spirit in you and give you life, now and forever. You're dead inside because of your sin, but you don't have to stay that way." Talk about good news that should bring great joy—this is it!

For many years, I was afraid of failing to please God. Jesus was my Savior, but I thought I had to do everything right, too. That was a lie from the pit of hell. I can't add a single thing to the blood of Jesus. His work on the cross was enough. My job is to believe this and be counted as righteous. Even the believing is a gift from Him. This is what I mean by walking in grace: knowing it is all a gift from Him, through His strength, and for His glory.

*Abba Father, thank You for sending Jesus to save us, redeem us, heal us, and set us free from every fear. Give us grace to believe the amazing truth that Jesus is our rest.* ♡

# *A Heart to Hear*

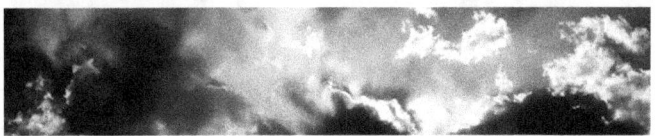

**DECEMBER 10 - 16**

## Reconciling The Vision

Have you ever noticed how the dream is always different from the reality? We imagine how things will be, but real life never follows the script, does it? We return home after a long absence only to find that some of the things that made us glad to leave haven't changed. Longing for the love of a romantic hero versus learning to get along with an actual flesh and blood man. By the time you find out he hits the snooze button five times every morning and hates to take out the trash, you're committed! How about newborn babies? All those Anne Geddes photos don't quite prepare you for the reality of walking the floor at two a.m. with a colicky infant, do they?

Surely many young girls in Israel dreamed of being chosen as the mother of Messiah. Just as surely, none of them ever dreamed the honor would include accusations of sexual immorality and being quietly "put away" by a fiancé who was too nice a guy to demand that she be stoned to death as the law allowed. Certainly those girls never imagined that the mother of Emmanuel would have to leave home and take a hard journey to a strange place where no familiar comfort could be found. They probably imagined this monumental event taking place in a palace surrounded by adoring hand maidens. No, the dream certainly didn't live up to the reality.

## *A Heart to Hear*

I'll never forget my first Christmas after giving birth. My heart broke for Mary as I considered her bearing the unpleasant parts of childbirth and its aftermath in the conditions she faced. I've never looked at a nativity scene the same way since!

Reconciling the vision with the actual events as they unfold is never easy. Our expectations keep tripping us up, don't they? However, I'm beginning to see that whether or not things ever turn out like I thought they would, I still want to dream. I still want God to show me visions. I still want to say to Him, like Mary, "Be it unto me according to Your word."

I don't understand all the things that God allows. I can't get my head around why He heals sometimes. I don't know why He allows hurt, betrayal, and loss to be part of our lives. Still, at the core, I know that His heart toward us is love. Even when we are in the fire, He is in there, too. When we grieve, it is not as beasts who must simply endure, but it is with hope that the One Who gave us life has something better. One day the reality will exceed the dream. One day all that we can think or imagine will be blown out of the water by the amazing reality of seeing and knowing Him as He really is.

*Abba Father, please help us hold on to You no matter what. Keep our hearts open to You even when we don't understand why. We love you, Lord. We bless Your name. You alone are good. Thank You for sending Jesus to save us, redeem us, and heal our hurting hearts.* ♡

Study: Psalm 84:5-7, 10-11

## *A Heart to Hear*

**DECEMBER 17 - 23**

# Prepare Him Room!

"Let every heart prepare Him room!" This phrase from the beloved Christmas carol, "Joy to the World," has been echoing in my head for several weeks now. Preparing Him room has captured my imagination.

Last week, my father came to visit. Preparing him a room involved giving my son a cleaning ultimatum, as his room became the guest room, buying new sheets for the bed, and tidying up the entire house. Thankfully, it did not involve the traditional freak-out I formerly engaged in whenever my parents came for a visit. When my oldest daughter was eight, she observed this behavior and remarked, "Mom, they raised you. They know you're not perfect!" Twelve years later, I know the truth: my dad loves me, and when he comes to visit, it isn't for inspection. Hallelujah! There is redemption in the house!

When it comes to preparing room for the King of kings, many of us react in the same manner. We think we need to clean and scour our hearts, put a shine on our spirits, and tidy up our lives. The sad thing is that Jesus came for the sole purpose of making all that obsolete. It's the difference between the law and grace. Under the law, the Old Covenant, it was all about keeping every rule and offering a sacrifice every time

## *A Heart to Hear*

you broke one. The good news of the New Covenant is that Jesus became the One and Only Sacrifice needed for ALL of our sin. All that is necessary for us to be made righteous is to believe He is the Saving One and open the door to receive Him. Jesus says, "Behold, I stand at the door and knock. If anyone hears My voice and opens the door, I will come in to him and eat with him, and he with Me" (Rev. 3:20).

Preparing Him room is as simple as opening the door and saying, "Yes, Lord, come into this messy stable that is my life," and allowing Him to do so. He knows how to clean us up, restore us, heal us, and make our lives about more than just trying to keep the rules.

Rejoice! The Savior is come! Open your heart, and receive Him with joy. You will never be the same!

*Abba Father, please open our hearts to receive You, and everything You have for us. Please help us absorb the wonder and awe of the fact that You came to us as a baby to show us Your love and set us free. Help us see how glorious You truly are! In Jesus' name. Amen.* ♡

## *A Heart to Hear*

**DECEMBER 24 - 31**

# Saying "Goodbye" Is a Gift

This morning I woke up with this thought in my head: *saying goodbye is a gift.*

As I've prayed about what the Lord is saying to us in this final week of the year, this is what is on my heart. I don't want to elaborate too much on this simple phrase—at best, it will sound like a high school graduation speech, and at worst, I will say something the Lord didn't intend. Therefore, let me just share the few clear impressions I have.

Saying a truly good "goodbye" means letting go with a blessing. It means acknowledging all the good that has gone before but realizing that a new chapter is beginning for everyone. Saying goodbye means it is now time to say hello to something new.

Even when saying goodbye is painful, there is blessing because the pain means what you've had is so precious it is hard to release.

The best part of all about goodbyes is that for believers in Jesus, they are always temporary. No goodbye between saints is ever permanent.

This year has been a year of goodbyes for all of us. Dearly loved people have left our presence for the presence of the Lord. Friends have moved to new places. Children have grown

## A Heart to Hear

up and left the nest. Situations have changed. Things will never be exactly the same, but in God's grace, every change we have experienced can be a new opportunity for Him to show Himself strong in our lives.

*Abba Father, please comfort our hearts in the difficult goodbyes. Give us grace to trust You when You open new doors for people we love. Comfort our hearts as we eagerly await reunions with those we cherish. Most of all, please open our hearts to fully embrace the new beginnings You have for us in the coming year. We love You, and we trust You. In Jesus' name. Amen.* ♡

www.ingramcontent.com/pod-product-compliance
Lightning Source LLC
LaVergne TN
LVHW051843080426
835512LV00018B/3047